Apache Country

A Cambodian Odyssey

CW5 Craig J. Houser (Ret)

Trenton, Georgia

Print ISBN: 978-1-958889-22-0
Ebook ISBN: 979-8-88531-468-8

Published by BookLocker.com, Inc., Trenton, Georgia, U.S.A.

Printed on acid-free paper.

Library of Congress Cataloguing in Publication Data
Houser (Ret), CW5 Craig J.
Apache Country: A Cambodian Odyssey by CW5 Craig J. Houser (Ret),
Library of Congress Control Number: 2023903097

BookLocker.com, Inc.
2023

ACKNOWLEDGEMENTS

I want to thank the following people, in no particular order, for their help throughout the years and their support of this endeavor:

Colonel James Kurtz has continuously helped me (and many others). He and I have been in contact with each other for many years. We have shared our memories of our time spent in Apache, the Cambodian "incursion," and the war in general. The last time we actually met in person, was in May of 2008, in Washington, DC, at the Vietnam Veterans Memorial, better known as "The Wall." We were in front of Panel 4W below the names of Curtis Smoot and Robert Kiser. That is also where most of our other friends are located.

My children for their support and encouragement and particularly my oldest son for continuing to "pressure" me to "finish the book."

My former colleague, Mr. Keith Perin, a high school English and Literature teacher, for helping me my with lack of grammar skills. He did the proof reading. I also want to thank his wife Kim, for putting up with my constant phone calls.

Vietnam veteran and author, Kregg P.J. Jorgenson (you need to read his books) for his friendship, encouragement, advice, support, and his knowledge about how to get something published.

My first wife, Dianne, for all the things she did to help me in those first months and years after returning from Vietnam. It could not have been easy for her, helping me with bad dreams and nightmares, putting up with my quick temper, and my smoking. She later told me how she and her mother had shared these same problems. Her father was an Army combat engineer in Europe in World War II. He never talked about it with his wife and children, but he told me his unit built the first pontoon bridge across the Rhine. Under heavy fire, they lost a lot of men; the wounded often fell into the river and were swept away. They completed the bridge.

Dedication

Sergeant Curtis R. Smoot

Missing In Action – Presumed Dead

10 Mar 1971

Specialist Four Robert T. Kiser

Killed In Action

10 Mar 1971

Table of Contents

Part I

10 March 1971

Day One

Chapter One

March the 10th, 1971, began like all the other days since we had started the Cambodian Offensive more than two weeks before. We had been “asked” by our Squadron commander to give 100% support for a three-to-five day clean-up operation inside the Cambodian border.

My unit, Troop A, 1st Squadron, 9th Cavalry Regiment, of the 1st Air Cavalry Division (Airmobile), was to operate in the vicinity of the Cambodian village of Snuol.

North Vietnamese divisions were operating inside Cambodia with little or no resistance from the Cambodian Army. These divisions had crossed into Laos north of the Demilitarized Zone and moved south along the Ho Chi Minh Trail system until they were in the southern part of Cambodia, not far from the South Vietnamese border. From here they were staging raids into South Vietnam and supplying the Viet Cong with equipment. All of this under the protection of the American policy of not “escalating” or expanding the war outside of Vietnam. Containment was the name of the game.

All of this changed, however, when President Richard Nixon allowed American forces to invade Cambodia for the first time in May and June of 1970. The invasion had lasted only two months (Nixon had promised that it would be a “limited” invasion). Nevertheless, the invasion was deemed to be a success; many of the Viet Cong and North Vietnamese regulars were killed, and much of their equipment was either captured or destroyed.

But that was back in June. As soon as American forces withdrew from Cambodia, the NVA and VC began to rebuild, unmolested by the Americans.

The American people played a big part in the present politics of the war. Nixon had been persecuted because of the misunderstanding on the part of the American people that this was an "escalation" of the war. Nixon had just announced previous to the invasion that the United States was de-escalating and withdrawing from Southeast Asia. The American people did not understand. Demonstrations and marches erupted all over the United States particularly on college campuses, most notably the tragedy at Kent State University in Ohio.

The paradox of the situation now was that the South Vietnamese could only survive an American pullout if they would not be faced with an immediate North Vietnamese offensive striking from their newly rebuilt Cambodian sanctuaries.

In other words, in order to have a successful de-escalation and pullout, we had to have a temporary escalation. We had to knock out those sanctuaries to literally give the South Vietnamese a fighting chance when the day came that we were no longer there to defend them.

So we were going back into Cambodia. But this invasion would be handled a little bit differently for the sake of President Nixon's image and the American perception of the war via the media. The announced and the publicized policy of the United States Military was that "we now have no United States ground forces in Cambodia." The key term here being "ground" forces. American pilots and aircrews were flying their butts off supporting ARVN (the Army of the Republic of Vietnam; the South Vietnamese Army) ground forces.

I suppose technically the administration was telling the truth. We were not *ground* forces. But the technicality was, of course, missed by the American people, as the Pentagon and the Nixon Administration knew it would be. As far as the American people were concerned, we had no American military forces in Cambodia, - - period. A game of words.

A runner from flight operations woke me before dawn.

"Mr. Houser. Mr. Houser. It's time to get up. Briefing in five minutes. It's time to get up, Mr. Houser."

By now he was shaking me.

"Alright, alright, for Christ's sake! I'm awake, I'm awake already! Jesus!"

I was awake now but I was numb. I had not slept well. In fact, I could not remember the last time I had slept well. The tension and anxiety of Cambodia was beginning to take its toll, not just on me but on everyone. The "three-to-five day" invasion was going into its third week now, and no one knew how much longer it would go on.

I think that is what bothered us as much as anything: not knowing how much longer that we had to endure and survive.

When this campaign started, we were told that it would not last longer than five days. And that when this excursion into Cambodia was over, our unit would "stand down." In other words, we would turn over our helicopters and our equipment either to another American aviation unit or to the ARVN, and our unit would go home. Of course, that did not insure that all of us would go home with it, but those of us with enough time "in country" would. We were never told what "enough time" was.

The aircraft were losing the battle for survival. We had gone into this thing with the understanding that it would not last any longer than five days, a week at the most. Routine maintenance procedures, such as oil changes and preventive maintenance replacement of parts, had been forgone in order to have full participation of flyable aircraft.

But now, after two weeks, with almost every aircraft behind on some sort of maintenance, everything was coming due at the same time. We were flying aircraft that we would not normally have flown (except in an emergency). But in the back of our minds, we knew that it would be over tomorrow or the next day. So what the hell, we could last another couple of days. After all, when this was over, we would "stand down," and a lot of us would be going home. The aircraft that survived would be parceled out to other American and ARVN aviation units and would become their "hangar queens" for a few weeks (or months) while they got all the parts and maintenance that they needed. Or they would be cannibalized for parts to keep other aircraft flying.

By the time I got to the briefing, it had already started with the same bullshit as the last several days; the AO (Area of Operation) would be the Snuol area. However we would be going farther north of Snuol than any of us had ever been. Three "pink teams,' each made up of a Cobra gunship and a LOH (Low observation helicopter; pronounced Loach) would leave at dawn followed by the Lift Platoon. The Lift Platoon Hueys would carry the Blues, our own internal infantry platoon. We would once again stage out of Loc Ninh, a small rubber plantation village just a few klicks (kilometers) this side of the border.

The Blues were not allowed to go in on the ground in Cambodia. They would stay behind at Loc Ninh in case of some kind of emergency on the South Vietnam side of the border. Our faithful, reliable Hueys would instead carry unfaithful, unreliable ARVN's (the Browns) into Cambodia and set them on the ground when and if we found something that we needed to look at up close. Or, more realistically, the very likely prospect of a downed aircraft. Assuming, of course, that we would be able to get the ARVN's off the aircraft once we were in Cambodia. They did not seem to care much for the war.

The briefing continued; pilots were assigned aircraft. Cobra pilots and Scout pilots were matched up to make "pink" teams. I would fly with 27. (pronounced two-seven).

Pilots, commanders, and units are reduced to numbers and code names in the military. It was a very simple system, one that I am sure the gooks had mastered for some time.

The White Platoon "Scout" Pilots were numbered from ten to nineteen; one-one, one-two, one-three, and so on. The Red Platoon "Gun" Cobra pilots were numbered from twenty to twenty-nine: two-one, two-two, two-three, etc. "Lift" platoon Huey pilots, "The Headhunters," were numbered from thirty to thirty-nine.

Platoon leaders were usually not referred to by their numbers but by their color. Thus, the Scout Platoon leader was referred to as "White" and the Gun Platoon leader as "Red." The Lift Platoon leader was referred to as three-zero since the name "Blue" was reserved for the platoon leader of our internal infantry platoon the "Blues."

Numbers and call signs had become such a way of life that we not only used the terms on the radio, but also in every day conversation. Other than my hootch mates and closest friends, everyone else referred to me as 12, or more formally, as Apache 12.

And that is the way I wanted it. There is psychological security that comes from a feeling of belonging, being a part of the team. And having a recognized call sign was the best way here to be a part of the team. One of the proudest days of my life was when I was given my call sign: Apache 12. I felt as though I had been knighted.

But a lot of responsibility came with that call sign, particularly for someone twenty years old. I knew I was young, most of us were.

Although Troop "A" in the Army scheme of things would normally be pronounced phonetically "Alpha" Troop, everyone in the squadron referred to us as Apache Troop. The 9th Cavalry Regiment had a long history that dated back to fighting the Plains Indians in the American West, the old 9th and 10th Cavalry "Buffalo Soldiers,"

It was a long and proud heritage. One of the most prized possessions of any Cav Trooper was his Stetson, which we wore proudly. All of us had our rank and the crossed sabers of the 1st of the 9th centered on the front. Commissioned Officers wore gold braided cords with matching acorns on the ends. Warrant Officers wore silver, and NCOs and enlisted wore yellow cotton cords.

After that, it was up to our own individuality as to what we did with it. Troopers molded, shaped, and formed their Cav hats to fit their own style and personality. Some wore it like a cowboy hat with the brim rolled up on the sides. Mine had what I called the "Scout droop". The brim was bent down low in the front and back. I had an OH-6 pin on one side and a First Team 1st Cav pin on the other side.

Bob Spencer pushed the crease in the center of the crown out along with the dents in the sides so that his hat was totally round. He looked like Tom Laughlin in *Billy Jack.* George Bullis had the front brim of his hat bent flat against the crown with his crossed sabers holding it in place. The enlisted troopers got even more creative with peace signs and love beads.

After the briefing, I went back to my hootch to get my helmet and the rest of my gear. My roommate, Bob Spencer and I had managed to grab this place a week before when Apache Troop had moved to Phuoc Vinh. Song Be was not much, but it had been home for Spencer and me for the seven months we had been in Vietnam. Home is what you get used to, the familiar. And although we needed the change, we hated to leave it. I think that most of the rest the troop hated to leave Song Be. We had lived there a long time and had made it as comfortable as possible.

In contrast, this hootch was more representative of what a hootch should be. It was an actual wooden structure. The 2 x 4 frame had wooden slats on the outside of the walls with the 2 x 4 studs exposed on the inside. There was no insulation from the heat. The tin roof kept most of the rain out, and we did not have to share it with anyone else. But it was new to us and therefore unfamiliar and somehow unfriendly.

Spencer was gone. He had come down with malaria and was now in the hospital in Long Binh. Like most of us, he had not been taking his malaria pills. We were given a small white pill to take every day and a big red one to take on Mondays. Since most of us suffered from chronic diarrhea, the added insult to our digestive tract of the big red pill was more than we could take. It only made the diarrhea worse. I don't think that any of us actually took the damn things. I know I didn't. Even though we swore in writing that we did.

The enlisted men's hootches were on the other side of the latrines. I walked into the Scout Platoon hootch and made my way through the dark to the acetate chart that showed the day's crew assignments. Next to my aircraft, 273, were written the names "Bennett" and "Smith". Smith was a new Oscar (observer) inexperienced in Scouts. He was one of the many new men who had come in to replace the guys we had lost in an ammo dump explosion at Song Be the night before our first day in Cambodia. That accident caused the death of Monty Harbin, a great guy and a good friend. It also cost us a large number of other highly experienced Scout door gunners and observers.

Bennett was an experienced Torque (door gunner) and crew chief. In fact, he used to be my door gunner. But we stopped getting along when he decided he knew more about flying Scouts than I did and that he should be in command of the aircraft. He fired on individuals without asking permission, dropped frag grenades when I wanted incendiaries, and seemed to do anything and everything he could to irritate me.

His biggest sin of all however, was that he was not conscientious in taking care of the aircraft. He gave it no more attention and respect than one would give to an old beat up farm truck.

I did not want Bennett today, and I damn sure did not want Smith; Cambodia was not the place for on-the-job training. I still hoped this would be over in a couple of days and he could learn the ropes in

Vietnam fighting mainly VC and not hard core NVA. The Viet Cong would often shoot at the aircraft and then run and hide. The North Vietnamese did not run.

For some reason my usual crewmembers, Curtis Smoot and Robert Kiser were not scheduled to fly at all today. After stumbling around in the dark with my Zippo lighter, I finally found Smoot.

"Smoot, wake up. Smoot, …come on, let's go," I said, as I looked for Kiser.

"Hey, Mr. Houser, I didn't think I had to fly today."

"Come on, let's go. I'll meet you at 273. Where is Kiser?"

After tripping over an M-60 and a flak jacket, I found Kiser in the opposite corner of the hootch.

"Kiser, wake up. I'll meet you at 273."

"Huh. What's going on?"

"Come on, get your shit and let's go."

I hated to make them fly today, but I hated to fly with someone I did not trust even more. Kiser and Smoot were experienced and I trusted them. They were my normally assigned crew. We had flown together for several months, and we worked well together.

The air outside the hootch smelled better than it did inside. The smell of sweaty bodies, dirty clothes, and stale farts gave way to the intolerable humidity of the early morning in Vietnam.

This was March, and by now we had entered the dry season. The unceasing downpours of the monsoons had ended some months before. Now we did not get enough rain to relieve the unbearable heat. It was stifling already, and the sun was not even up yet.

I decided that I had enough time for my usual cup of coffee before I went to the flight line, so I walked to the squadron mess hall.

It was far different from the tent that had served as Apache Troop's mess hall at Song Be. It had to be; after all, this was considered a "rear" area. The "brass" had to have a nice place to eat. We almost felt like intruders here. Milk in chilled coolers, eggs any way you wanted them. Real eggs, not powdered eggs.

This was a large steel beam building with a concrete floor. The walls were steel sided with no windows. Four large exhaust fans, two on each end of the building, moved the hot humid air around. Fiberglass tables and chairs made it resemble a school cafeteria or a factory break room except for the military crests, emblems, and flags decorating the walls.

I got two paper cups, one inside the other, poured myself some coffee, decided to pass on the eggs, and headed for the flight line. Other pilots and crews were beginning to do the same.

Shadowy figures walked in twos and threes down the long line of revetments. Beams of light from their flashlights bounced around as they walked, unable to penetrate the heavy mist, as men peered into dark revetments searching for tail numbers or anything that they would recognize as their aircraft.

The airframes were just beginning to become visible to me, still shapeless in the distance, as I walked down the long flight line. I knew where I had parked 273 the day before, but nothing looked right in the dark.

I could not help thinking what it must be like to stay here in Phuoc Vinh every day. The relative security of squadron headquarters was represented by the mess hall. There was not a single sandbag anywhere around the building. Not one.

That is not to say that it was safe here. The first night I ever spent in Phuoc Vinh, the compound took a direct hit with a 122 mm rocket. I had flown our Troop commander, Major Harris, down to Phuoc Vinh from Song Be for some kind of a meeting. It turned out that he would be staying for the night, so I had to find a place to stay. I ended up sleeping in my classmate Tommy Pepper's hootch and was introduced to his hootchmate Bruce Campbell. They were both Charlie Troop Scout pilots.

We had been playing cards with some other guys when I decided to get rid of some beer.

I stepped outside of the hootch and was taking a leak under a nearby tree when the rocket came in. I had never experienced "In Coming" before. I barely heard it come in, but I certainly heard the impact when it took out the commo tower. This was not the troop or squadron tower; this was the tall orange and white communications tower for the entire FSB (fire support base).

I ran back in the hootch, and the room was empty; they had crawled down into a bunker underneath the floor. Tommy was calling to me to get in there with them.

I yelled, "Do you get this a lot?"

"Yeah, we get mortars from time to time," Bruce said.

"Well, this was no mortar," I yelled back.

We waited for more rockets, but there were none; Charlie was done for the night. Just the one rocket and a perfect direct hit.

In a way, I envied the rear area cooks, clerks, and mechanics. They had no idea what it was like to be afraid. They had never been shot at and never would be. Other than the occasional mortars and maybe a rocket, their war was boredom. They would never know what it was like to force themselves to go out on missions day after day. Missions that did not seem to accomplish a thing. The constant knot in their stomach endlessly churning.

I felt sick to my stomach as I did now every morning before a flight. I did not used to be this way before a mission, but for the last several weeks, maybe even months, I felt like this every morning. I knew that I was not physically ill, although the physical signs of illness were real enough. I had been vomiting almost every morning on the flight line for some time now. That's why I did not eat anything in the mess hall this morning. I knew I would lose it.

But I knew the source of the illness was not some mysterious Asian disease. It was not malaria or encephalitis. It was not VD or even the water. No, it was something much worse. Something that I could not take medicine for. Something I would have to fight on my own. It was the constant gripping fear. The fear of dying in this God forsaken place. Or, even worse than dying, being captured or burning to death in a crash after being shot down.

I did not know how the other guys handled their fears. We never talked about it. Oh, we talked about various different scenarios of being shot at, hit, and even going down. But we never actually discussed fear itself.

We often discussed the source of our fears, especially once we started the Cambodian offensive. The .51 caliber machine guns that could reach up and zap you at 3500 feet or more. The 37 mm anti-aircraft guns that the NVA were rumored to have brought down from the North. Heat seeking, shoulder fired missiles, also rumored to have been brought south. B-40 and RPG's (rocket propelled grenades) particularly deadly to low flying scout birds. Mechanical disasters such as engine failures, main rotor separation, and fire. We talked about all these fears and others, but we never really discussed fear itself, or how to deal with it.

We each fought this battle inside ourselves in our own separate ways. Some of us handled it better than others. Some did not handle it very well at all. All of us drank. Almost all of us smoked cigarettes. And I knew one or two pilots in my troop that smoked dope, but that was very rare for pilots, and they did it at night when they were very sure they would not have a mission. Among the Scout enlisted men it was much more common.

As far as regular cigarettes, we could get all the major American brands at the PX (post exchange) for $1.70 a carton. I smoked Marlboros and was now up to three packs a day.

But for those cooks, clerks, and mechanics (who were not crew chiefs) who would never see what we saw, who would never experience what we experienced, who would never hear a shot fired in anger, and who would only hear stories about the war, for them, their war was fought against boredom. That was their curse, and they envied us.

Chapter Two

The first hint of dawn cast its hazy red glow on the horizon as I reached my aircraft. I found 273 parked where I had left her in a protective revetment. About half of our LOHs were in revetments, and the others were out in the open unprotected.

Now that we were sharing Pinetree, the squadron parking area, there were not enough revetments to go around. Charlie Troop (C Troop) had always been here in Phuoc Vinh, or at least since I arrived in country in August 1970. Apache Troop added roughly thirty additional aircraft to an already crowded flight line. Headquarters Troop was also here, but they had very few aircraft and no Cobras or LOHs.

My pre-flight inspection of 273 progressed quickly; I had done this same inspection on her so many times I knew what to spend time looking at and what not to worry about. We were old friends. She had been assigned to me since my arrival in the troop. We had shared a myriad of experiences together. Some of the experiences had been exciting, some had been humorous, others tragic, but they were always exhilarating, always fascinating; the miracle of flight combined with the excitement and thrill of danger.

I finished the outside inspection, noting that some of the rivets on the skids were loose, and climbed into the right seat. The instrument panel on an OH-6A is very basic. The bare necessities, and I mean *bare*. But it's adequate. I started through my cabin checklist, which I had long before committed to memory. Cyclic control -- neutral; collective pitch -- full down; throttle -- set; radios -- off; lights -- off. Smoot showed up with his gear.

"Where the hell's Kiser?" I asked, concentrating on my procedure.

"He said he had to go to the latrine, Mr. Houser. I think he's got the runs or something."

"Well, he better get his ass down here, we gotta get goin'."

I did not see 27, but I figured he was about to crank, and I was already beginning to hear the high pitch whine of Lycoming turbines of Hueys and Cobras coming to life. Smoot was checking his ammo box, counting and sorting grenades.

Clock -- set; altimeter -- set to field elevation; compass -- check; circuit breakers -- in.

"That damn M-60 of yours gonna work today?" I asked, commenting on Smoot's machine gun. It was notorious for jamming.

"I think so, Mr. Houser," Smoot said, in his deep Southern drawl. "I took it all apart again last night, changed the firing pin, put on a different barrel, and cleaned and oiled it, - everything."

Inverter -- off; generator -- off; fuel pump -- off; scav air -- off; fuel valve -- check.

"Well, I tell you Curtis. If you don't get that son-of-a-bitch fixed, I'm gonna throw you both out at about two thousand feet. You know that gun is gonna get us in a real trick bag one of these days."

"I know it, Mr. Houser. I work on it back in the hootch almost every night. Then we get out flying; and it fucks up. I don't know why it does that. I swear I keep it clean and everything."

"I believe you, Curtis. Just do the best you can with it. But you have got to tell me the instant that the damn thing jams, so that I know that we don't have a gun. Don't start working on it without telling me that you can't fire. And for Christ's sake, don't beat the butt of the gun on the floorboard without telling me first that you're gonna do it. That scares the shit out of me every time that you do that."

"I know. O.K."

Bypass air -- check; battery switch -- on; engine out audible -- check; caution and warning lights -- check; press to test -- check. I put my helmet and gloves on. I was ready to crank. Kiser ran up and climbed in the left seat.

"Where have you been?" I asked, as I tightened my chinstrap.

"I had to go to the latrine. Twice."

"Well, are you gonna be alright? It's going to be awhile till we get you to the next latrine."

"I'll be alright."

"O.K., but I don't think I've got any toilet paper, and it's going to be a while before we get somewhere that we can actually land."

"I'll be O.K. Really."

I set the throttle again, turned my head as far as I could to my left and right to clear myself; and yelled "clear!"

Smoot was standing out in front of the aircraft at the twelve o'clock position holding the fire extinguisher. He yelled "clear!" to affirm that I was in fact clear of any obstructions or personnel, and with his left hand holding the fire bottle, swung his right hand and arm above his head in a large circle.

I pushed the starter button, watched the gauges for a response, and at the same time watched to see that the rotor blades were beginning to turn. The Allison engine started its high pitch whine, and the gauges began to come to life. I monitored the TOT (turbine outlet temperature) closely for a "hot" start. The needles of the dual engine and rotor tachometer were climbing. I twisted the throttle, and the whine changed to an explosion as the engine RPM increased with the sudden introduction of more fuel.

Smoot fastened the Velcro straps of his "chicken plate," plugged in his helmet, and climbed aboard, sitting directly behind me on the right side.

"All set, Mr. Houser!"

"Swell," I said, concentrating on the TOT gauge. I also noted the crank time.

Generator switch -- on; inverter -- set; gyro -- pull; radios – on; throttle – full open; engine oil pressure – check.

Then I saw a blink, a yellow caution light came on. It was a chip detector caution light.

"Shit," I said over the intercom, "We've got a chip light." It could be any one of three. This was the tail rotor.

"What's the matter, Mr. Houser?" asked Smoot.

"We've got a tail rotor chip light on."

The chip detector lights were wired to magnetic sensors located in the bottom of the engine, main rotor transmission, and the tail rotor transmission. Oil circulates around these magnetic plugs, which look similar to spark plugs. A light coming on usually indicates that the "gap" in the plug has been "closed" by fine metal particles from normal gear wear. Attracted to the magnet, the particles will eventually close the gap completing the electrical circuit, which brings the light on.

Most of the time when the plug is pulled, the crew chief will find fine metal fillings, which have to be checked by maintenance personnel. They clean the "fuzz" off the plug, reinstall it, and if the light stays off, we are on our way. On the other hand, sometimes they pull the plug and find larger pieces of metal, even chunks, which indicate that a gear is disintegrating.

If you have broken pieces of gears in there, it becomes a serious problem fast. It is only a matter of time before the gearbox (or engine) fails. Maintenance has the final say as to what is fuzz and what is bigger than fuzz. It cannot be a pilot or crew chief decision.

Taking this problem to its full extent, a broken piece of gear lodged in just the right place could cause the gearbox to actually explode. Or the housing to crack and the resulting loss of fluid cause the gearbox to get hot and "freeze" up.

Either way, the loss of a tail rotor in flight was not a pleasant thought. An emergency landing with no tail rotor is tricky, especially in an LOH. There is also the problem of the loss of CG (center of gravity). If the tail rotor transmission actually does explode and falls off, the resulting loss of the weight of the transmission stuck clear out there on the end of the tail boom, causes the aircraft to go into an uncontrollable nose dive. There is absolutely no way to regain control. Game over.

I tapped the light with my finger. I had a feeling this was not a short in the wiring, although I had never had a chip light come on in 273.

By now other pink teams were hovering out of the parking area to take the active runway to take off. They would fly as a group to Loc Ninh. I had to get another aircraft, and that would take time. I checked my FM radio to make sure that it was on Alpha Troop's current frequency. Flight Operations had to know that I had to have another aircraft.

"Rigid Tiger Four-Zero, this is Apache One-Two. Rigid Tiger Four-Zero, this is Apache One-Two." Come on, I said to myself, impatient now to get going.

"Apache One-Two, this is Rigid Tiger Four-Zero, go ahead."

"Roger, Four-Zero, One-Two has a broken aircraft. Get a hold of my Poppa Sierra and get me another one ASAP, Over."

Radio procedure was such that actual names were never mentioned over the air. In the phonetic alphabet, Poppa Sierra, or PS, referred to my platoon sergeant who would now have to release another aircraft to me since mine was "down". I would also need that logbook as soon as possible.

"Roger, One-Two, understand you need replacement aircraft."

"Yes, roger that, and I need it ASAP," I said, as I shut down 273. I had plenty of battery if I did not have to leave the radio on much longer without the engine running.

After about a two minute pause, the voice finally came back, "Roger, One-Two, you can take aircraft five five five, over."

We did not have a 555, or at least we did not have an OH-6 that was a 555. Damn it.

"Negative Four-Zero, Triple Nickel is a UH-1, I need an OH-6," I said with obvious disgust. "Find my Poppa Sierra." Another long pause.

This confusion was partially caused by the fact that Apache Troop was sharing the flight operations center with squadron and with Charlie Troop.

I went ahead and called 27.

"Apache Two-Seven, this is One-Two on fox (FM), you copy all this?"

"Roger, One-Two, I'm going ahead on up," said 27. (Carl Rosepepe)

"O.K., Two-Seven, I'll catch up as soon as I can. If possible, let my platoon leader know what's going on."

"One-Two, this is Four-Zero, cannot find your Poppa Sierra."

"Roger. One-Two out," I said, as I realized this was going to take more time than I had thought. I turned off the radio and the battery.

The blades had long since stopped and Kiser and Smoot were out of the aircraft standing next to my door. I took off my helmet and gloves.

"We're gonna have to find SSG Schmitt. You guys know where he sleeps?"

"I think he's in with Sgt. Wheeler, but I'm not sure," said Smoot. "That's the hootch behind ours."

"O.K., well, you go find him. Tell him I need a replacement aircraft right away and the logbook as soon as I can get it."

Staff Sergeant Leonard G. Schmitt was Apache Troop's new Scout Platoon Sergeant. He had only been with us for a few weeks, but he was a good man. He was one of the few "lifers" that I really truly liked and respected. He reminded me of the Marlboro Man: 6'2"or 3", stocky, well tanned, and weathered looking,with a thick reddish-brown mustache waxed and curled at the ends. He really did look like he had just walked right off a Marlboro billboard. In reality, he had come to us from the infantry. He had no aviation experience or background.

Even though with that mustache he looked like he could have been a warrant officer, he came from a world where there were almost no warrant officers, into a world where almost all the aviators were warrants. Moreover, he could not quite figure us out. Most of us were 19 or 20. Most of us had only been in the Army the length of time that it took to go through basic training and flight school. Most of us did not want to be in Vietnam and were not going to make the Army a career.

We were a paradox to SSG Schmitt and the other NCOs (noncommissioned officers/ E-5 and above). They had known old NCO's, E-8s and E-9s, who had gotten their warrant appointment the "old" way as a reward for long time service, being at the top of the enlisted ranks, and for their expertise and professionalism. Vietnam changed all that. Those warrants were still around, but now most warrants were in aviation.

The World War II days of the "flying sergeants" were over. You now had to be an officer to be an aviator in the Army. However, the Army did not necessarily need you to be a lieutenant or a captain; a warrant officer would do fine. So the Army created the Warrant Officer Flight Program. Flight school was almost a year long, not counting basic training. The Army needed helicopter pilots,......a lot of helicopter pilots. Long time Army experience was not necessary. Neither was college. You only needed to be a high school graduate to be eligible for the Army Warrant Officer Flight Program. Unlike the other branches of the military, a college degree was not a prerequisite. After a little over a year in the program, the Army graduated a class of rotary wing aviators every two weeks, mainly warrant officers. We received our WO1 bar on one day and the following day received our wings (along with our orders for Vietnam).

I really liked SSG Schmitt, but I doubted that he liked me very much. The first or second week that he was with us, he and I had had a disagreement over the painting of the numbers on some of the aircraft. I had painstakingly painted 273's numbers and troop and squadron insignia on her myself some months before. I had to get yellow paint from the village, all we had was white. I had also painted the skid "toes." It looked good and I was proud of it.

In an effort as a new platoon sergeant to keep the men busy and to do something constructive, SSG Schmitt had detailed some to the Scouts to repaint all the aircraft numbers. The aircraft numbers were displayed on OH-6's on the nose and just forward of the tail boom below the masthead. The numbers were painted in yellow (if we could find it) for the Cavalry. In the true spirit of the Army, "If it moves, salute it; if it doesn't, paint it," he had ordered all the aircraft numbers repainted regardless of how good they already looked or how recently they had been done. Realizing that this was just busy work, the guys had not put much effort into it and had done a pretty sloppy job. To top it off, they only had white paint.

I do not remember exactly what I had said to SSG Schmitt, but the gist of the conversation was that 273 did not belong to the United States Army, she belonged to me. If there was any doubt in his mind about this he should look at the *12* painted inside the yellow triangle below the masthead. The yellow triangle meant that the aircraft belonged to Apache Troop and the 12 meant that that particular aircraft belonged to me. I would decide when and if she needed paint. If I wanted something painted on her, I would do it myself. In the meantime, I did not want another paintbrush on the aircraft without asking me first. It was ugly. It was ugly and immature.

The rest of the conversation, if you could call it that, was just as narrow minded and obnoxious. To make matters worse, in the heat of my anger, I had confronted Schmitt in front of some of the other scouts.

It embarrasses me now to even think about it. He was a good guy trying to do his job, and I was an immature dumbass. I hated that I had acted so stupidly.

What SSG Schmitt did not understand, not having been around aviation before, was that these aircraft were not jeeps or tanks. We pilots truly cared for these aircraft. Most of us were very young, so we babied these helicopters as if they were the Chevys and Fords and motorcycles that we had left at home. We washed them, we tinkered with them, and we painted them as if they truly were our own.

By the time we had been given another aircraft (363) and had gotten it preflighted, the sun had risen considerably, and it was beginning to get hot. It was not our fault, but we had wasted a lot of time. We were scheduled to fly the second mission this morning. By now, the first team out in the AO (area of operation) would be coming back to Loc Ninh to refuel and rearm, and the second would be on the way out. I wondered who that would be since we were still in Phuoc Vinh. If we left right now, we could get there in time to refuel and make the third mission. I checked the UHF radio to make sure that it was on Phuoc Vinh tower's frequency and keyed the mike switch.

"Phuoc Vinh Tower, this is Apache three six three."

"This is Phuoc Vinh tower, go ahead three six three," the voice came back briskly.

"Roger, Phuoc Vinh. Three six three is a single LOH, Pinetree for hover departure north."

"Roger, three six three, winds three to five from the northeast, altimeter two-niner niner-two. You're clear to take the active, call hover check complete."

"Three six three."

I checked the RPM, pulled the collective pitch in slowly, and eased the left pedal forward. The aircraft began to get light.

"What's it look like back there, Smoot?"

"We're clear to the rear."

I pulled in more pitch. As the rotor system began to accept all the weight, the skids began to leave the ground and slid in towards each other. I slowly backed 363 out of the revetment.

An OH-6 is a very sensitive machine, especially at a hover. The unique tail assembly, a combination of a vertical and a diagonal stabilizer on the right side of the aircraft, causes the aircraft to sometimes be unpredictable at a hover. This situation is aggravated when you have a tailwind, especially from the right, of more than eight to ten knots. Add to this an overweight aircraft, high density altitude, and thin air, and you have your hands full.

As you roll in throttle and pull in pitch in the rotor blades, you must compensate for the increased torque by pushing in left pedal, which increases the pitch in the tail rotor, taking a bigger bite of air. Occasionally the air is so thin, due to the heat, that you actually "run out" of left pedal; the pedal is against the stop. Unable to compensate enough for the torque, the aircraft begins to spin to the right. This is not a serious problem if you have plenty of room. You simply roll off the throttle and perform a hovering autorotation. However, in a revetment, where the aircraft does not have enough room to turn around, you can screw up a good aircraft real fast.

Revetments for LOHs were parallel walls built out of PSP (pierced steel planks or perforated steel plating). Army engineers had built these short revetments for OH-6s and taller ones for the Hueys and Cobras. The Cobra revetments were shaped like an upside down "L." Our Cobras were always fully loaded with rockets, ammunition, and fuel. At that weight they could barely hover at all and could not back straight out of a revetment. The "L" shape allowed them to sort of slide to the side and rear at about a one or two inch hover.

The PSP formed an outside shell, which was filled usually with dirt or sometimes gravel.

The hope was that a Viet Cong rocket or mortar falling in between revetments would miss the aircraft. Or, if did hit one, the explosion of fire and shrapnel would not get the next aircraft in line. The walls were low enough to allow the rotor blades to droop without hitting them, but high enough to give reasonably good protection.

For a while we had a guy in the Scout Platoon named Charles Anderson. I could not take an aircraft out of a revetment without thinking about him and how *not* to do it. He was one of the first people I met when I came to Apache Troop and I knew that there was something odd about him right away. He came up to me on the flight line and introduced himself.

"Hi, I'm Charles Anderson. Nobody likes me."

He was right, and it did not take me long to find out why.

Anderson was the company "fuck-up." Every company and troop had one. He had come to Apache Troop after being transferred out of Charlie Troop. Charlie Troop got him after he was transferred out of the 229th. God knows where he was before that or how many units had dumped him. He was now in the Lift Platoon as a permanent co-pilot that nobody wanted. He would never be an AC (aircraft commander). He was resigned to spending his tour in Vietnam "watching the loadmeter" and not touching the controls.

Some months before, while trying to take a LOH out of a revetment, he had "lost" or run out of left pedal. Instead of "chopping" (reducing) the throttle and autorotating a foot to the ground, he had pulled full pitch and shot up spinning uncontrollably to about twenty feet. *Then* he decided to chop the throttle, whereupon he fell back into the revetment sideways, breaking off the tail boom and spreading the skids. Luckily no one was hurt, but his door gunner/crew chief was so angry that anyone could be that stupid that he almost shot him with his M-60. He would have had the full support of the Scout Platoon.

PT, or pilot technique, was something that you either had or you did not. Although it could be improved upon with practice, it could never really be learned from someone else. Charles Anderson would never have PT. The irony of the situation was that Anderson had survived this long in Vietnam in spite of himself, while much better pilots had been killed doing everything right. Victims of fate, I guess.

I wondered what had ever happened to Anderson. Another one of those guys that just kind of disappeared. Units got rid of those guys like people trade off a lemon of a car. Companies and troops would trade the biggest loser they had to another company for their loser and hope they got the better end of the deal.

I hovered out of Pinetree and on to the active.

"Phuoc Vinh Tower, three six three has a good hover check."

"Roger, three six three; you're clear. Check the Cobras on final."

"Roger, three six three is on the go," I said, as I watched two cobra gunships turn on final approach.

The ship was heavy with a full load of fuel, all of our equipment, and the three of us on board. In the early morning heat, I could only hover at twelve to eighteen inches. There were no flight school takeoffs in Vietnam. I eased the cyclic forward, building up speed inches off the ground. The skids brushed the runway once, and we were airborne. In seconds we had crossed the end of the runway, over the silent 105 mm batteries, and then the perimeter with its rows of concertina barbed wire. Phuoc Vinh and its relative security fell away quickly below us as we continued our climb to the north.

I switched the FM radio off of our troop operations frequency over to Phuoc Vinh artillery.

"Phuoc Vinh Arty, this is Apache One-Two. Phuoc Vinh Arty, Apache One-Two."

Sometimes they answered, and sometimes they didn't .

"This is Phuoc Vinh Arty, go ahead One-Two," the voice came back from a sleepy plotter.

"Roger, One-Two is Phuoc Vinh to Dong Xoai along the road. Over."

I related where I was, where I was going, and my planned route. I really should have used my tail number instead of my call sign, I thought to myself, this is not Song Be.

The policy was supposed to be to only use "family" (internal) call signs when we were talking to other aircraft or stations in Apache Troop, or, at least in the squadron, but to use the tail numbers (the last three numbers of the aircraft's registration number) when we made a call outside the family, (i.e., talking to an airfield control tower, checking with artillery, etc). But a lot of us used our personal call sign for everything, especially at Song Be where the tower operators recognized us. I should have used my tail number. "Oh, well, fuck it."

"Negative firing that sector, call Song Be Arty at Dong Xoai. Over."

"Thank you, Phuoc Vinh," I said, wondering if the guy had actually checked to make sure his artillery firing did not conflict with my route of flight. I did not need to fly through "friendly" artillery today.

"Hey, Mr. Houser," Smoot said over the intercom from directly behind me in the cargo bay. "You think that guy really checks that out when you call him?"

"I don't know, Curtis. I like to think so."

"Yeah, I was just wondering."

"So was I."

I did not think that artillery would be firing this early, but you only have to fly through it once to learn that it is worth a radio call.

I had flown through "friendly fire" some months earlier with 24 (CW2 Jerry Boyle). The 155s had been pounding a hillside for an hour, and we were supposed to go in and do a BDA (battle damage assessment). After confirming that the artillery was turned off, 24 put me down to work the area. I had just gotten down low level and started to work when a thundering "ka-boom" sent dust and debris flying to my right. I did not know what had happened. Then another "ka-boom," and then another, this time to my left.

"Holy shit, I thought you had that fucking artillery shut off!" I screamed into my mike. I pulled the collective pitch up in to my armpit and broke off to the east, while the Cobra broke north.

"I thought I had; they confirmed it!" replied an equally shrill scream from 24.

It was all a mistake; someone at division had gotten the word to start firing again, thinking that we had already finished in the area. Just a mistake. Sorry.

I switched the FM radio back to today's Apache Troop "family" frequency.

"Rigid Tiger Four-Zero, this is Apache One-Two."

"This is Four-Zero, go ahead, One-Two."

"Roger, Four-Zero, One-Two is off Phuoc Vinh enroute Loc Ninh."

"Roger, One-Two, got you off. Four-Zero out."

We settled back for the fifty minute flight to Loc Ninh.

Chapter Three

At two 2000 feet, the jungle below was a lush green carpet. It did not look menacing. Actually, it looked beautiful. Other than a slowly rising column of smoke to the west, there were no indications that there was a war going on down there.

I flew with the cyclic between my knees as I fumbled for a cigarette. We did not fly with doors on low-birds, and the wind whipping through the cockpit made it difficult to light one.

I had decided to fly to Loc Ninh by way of Song Be. I was not sure of the heading direct from Phuoc Vinh to Loc Ninh, and I did not have a map. So I would go the way that I was familiar with even though it was well out of the way. We would fly up the road from Phuoc Vinh to Dong Xoai. Here the road split with one branch going off to the northeast and the other to the northwest. We would leave the road at this point and go direct to Song Be. I could see the mountain already.

Nui Ba Ra stood alone as a single conical shaped mountain, rising 1500 hundred feet above the surrounding terrain. It was a perfect landmark in daylight. In good weather, from 2000 feet, it could be seen for 40 miles in any direction. At night or in bad weather, it posed a significant threat for someone trying to find his way home to Song Be.

I remembered what an impression the mountain had made on me the first time that I saw it. Standing alone, rising out of the jungle, the only mountain within sixty miles. Timeless, unconquerable, unchanging, a giant monument to its creator. All the years of conflict and war. First the Chinese; it took the Vietnamese a thousand years to get them out. Then the French, then the Japanese, then the French again, and now the Americans. The mountain had been there through it all. Now its thick jungle and caves hid the Viet Cong just as it had the Viet Minh.

Wc Amcricans had a small radio relay station on her summit, manned by about 15 men. The "friendlies" controlled the base of the mountain and supposedly regularly patrolled it. But the VC controlled her sides and knew her secrets. They hid in the caves and the thick vegetation of her slopes.

The Viet Cong, like the mountain and the jungle itself, seemed invincible. We fought them and killed them by the dozens and even by the hundreds, but there were always more. It was like killing ants in your backyard. They always came back, just like the jungle. No matter how much we blew it up, no matter how much of it we burned, it always came back just as thick as before. The VC were the same way: a part of the jungle.

At the base of Nui Ba Ra, on the northeast side, lay the village of Song Be. It was really more than just a village; it was actually a small town. When I think of a village, I think of a hamlet with ten or twelve hootches. Song Be was a good size town of several thousand people. From our position several miles to the south, the town was still hidden by the mountain, but I could see it clearly in my mind.

The Song Be River meandered down from the north, making several wide turns as it passed through the town. Most of the town was on the northeast side of the river. A large concrete and steel bridge connected the two parts of the town. Some of our Scout pilots, particularly Apache 11 (WO1 Bob Long) and Apache 18 (WO1 Stanley McCaw), occasionally tested their skill by flying under the bridge between its two large columns. So far, I had never been that confident of my abilities.

Below us now lay Dong Xoai, a small village halfway between the Mountain and Phuoc Vinh. Dong Xoai had been the site of a major battle a few years earlier. I changed my FM radio over to Song Be Arty, and verified that there was no firing going on in this sector between me and the mountain.

Normally the Cobra took care of all the administrative calls when we traveled together. He also had the map and the "whiz wheel," a round plastic code device made up of numbers and letters. The user rotated the outside wheel, which represented units, call signs, and frequencies. A disposable page was inserted and changed every day to keep up with the master codes, which changed every 24 hours. Usually the Cobra AC wore the whiz wheel around his neck on a dog tag chain. In the event that the wheel was lost or captured (if it was lost in a downed aircraft, it was assumed that it was captured), it would only be good to the enemy for the remainder of the time period, which ended at midnight.

At Dong Xoai the road split. The east fork curved around to the right and came into Song Be on the northeast side of the mountain. The west fork to the left formed a much larger arc through a burned out village that had once been a small rubber plantation. Then it slowly turned back to the northeast to eventually rejoin the other road at Song Be.

The elevation had changed considerably between Phuoc Vinh and here. Generally the further inland you went the higher the elevation. Phuoc Vinh was several hundred feet lower than Song Be. The terrain had changed also, from relatively flat land with a few rice paddies around Phuoc Vinh, to gently rolling land with thick forest in this area. Between here and Song Be the thick forest became mixed with thick jungle. The farther north you went, the thicker the jungle became.

The elevation here was too high for lowland rice. Much of the jungle was made up of hardwoods, and there were scattered logging operations in this area.

Song Be village was visible now; the checkerboard effect of the early morning sun on the metal roofs gave the town away. The Vietnamese could make anything out of anything. They had scrounged around the American bases taking odds and ends home with them.

Although their hootches were mainly constructed of wood and thatch work, they often repaired their roofs with pieces of tin and corrugated steel. From the air, a Vietnamese village looked like a shantytown, a Hooverville of the Depression Era.

On the northwest side of the mountain, and now directly in front of us, was Fire Support Base Buttons. To those of us who had lived there, this was Song Be. If, in conversation, we meant the town, we called it Song Be village. I was close enough now that I could swing around to the northwest and pick up a heading for Loc Ninh, but I could not resist flying over Song Be one last time. This had been where I had lived for my first seven months "in country,"

Apache Troop had pulled out of Song Be (FSB Buttons) shortly after we started the Cambodia mission. We were under the impression that the ARVNs were taking over the base immediately. In fact, we were under strict orders not to damage any of the hootches or buildings in our exit. Some of the guys could just not accept giving away to the ARVNs what they had worked so hard over the months to make livable.

Like Apache 24's (Jerry Boyle) famous bathtub. Well, maybe not famous, but it was well admired around Apache Troop. He had somehow built that tub out of a rubber mat on a 2 x 4 frame and plumbed it himself. Pilots tried to do whatever they could to get Jerry to let them try out that tub. We had showers, but no one but Jerry had a tub to soak in. I never did get to use it.

As a result of being ordered *not* to damage anything, there were hard feelings generated all around resulting in quite a bit of damage done when we left. Some people tore out electric lines, ripped doors off hootches, tore out handmade shelves fabricated from ammo boxes, and generally left the place a wreck. Regardless of the way that we left it, it would be much better than the South Vietnamese soldiers were used to and a damn sight better than what was here when we arrived.

Something was wrong, though. I could not see any movement on FSB Buttons, or any vehicles. I decided to go down to take a closer look. Something was different about it, and as we dropped through 1500 feet, it became painfully obvious what it was.

"Hey, take a look at the Apache AO," I said.

"I don't believe it, Mr. Houser, all the hootches are gone!" Smoot said in shock.

I did not believe it either, but it was true. Except for a few sections of galvanized steel lying around, every one of our hootches was gone!

We had lived in corrugated galvanized steel drainage culverts. We liked to say with a good amount of truth that we lived in sewer pipes. They were crude, but they were strong and relatively comfortable considering the way the grunts and some of the other units lived. We had added electricity from gasoline generators, which then allowed us to have lights and operate fans, radios, and even small refrigerators.

"That just shows how fucked up the gooks are," Smoot said in disgust.

It was not hard to figure out what had happened. We had pulled out and left the fire support base more or less intact, but before the ARVNs could take over the compound, the surrounding locals had stripped the place. "How the hell could they ever win the war if they could not even control their own people," I thought.

I made a slow turn to the northwest and noticed that the lookout towers and most of the other wooden structures were also gone. Even the airstrip control tower was gone. Hell, everything was gone! We had left them a perfectly good fire support base. All they had to do was move their people in to it. They could not even do that!

As resourceful as the local villagers were, it also occurred to me that something more sinister might also have happened. It could very well be that some South Vietnamese general decided to line his pockets by selling everything he could order his men to disassemble and remove, then blame it on local thieves and have the Americans rebuild it. It would not be the first time.

I once again made a radio call to Song Be Arty to see if there was any firing going on in this sector between Song Be and Loc Ninh. They said there was nothing. I changed the FM radio back to "family."

We had been flying for about 45 minutes since leaving Phuoc Vinh. Song Be was several miles behind us and the jungle below was thick and rugged. Suddenly a caution light flickered and then stayed on. It was the generator light. I tapped it with my finger; it stayed on.

"Fuck, this isn't our day," I said, as I keyed my mike switch.

"What's the matter, Mr. Houser?" Smoot asked.

"We've got a generator caution light on; I think we've lost the generator."

An OH-6 can continue to fly with no generator. We were about fifteen minutes out of Loc Ninh, and barring any other problems, we should not have any difficulty flying that short of a distance. Still, I would need to shut down as much of the electrical system as I could. That also meant that I had better make a radio call while I still could.

"Any Apache aircraft, this is Apache One-Two on Uniform," (UHF). I doubted that anyone would hear us. "Any Apache aircraft, this is Apache One-Two on Uniform."

"Go ahead, One-Two; this is Apache Three-Eight."

Max Evans, you sweetheart, I thought to myself.

"Roger, Three-Eight, One-Two is enroute Loc Ninh. Please advise the family that we have a generator failure. We'll be turning electrical systems off. Estimate Loc Ninh to be about fifteen minutes. We are east of Loc Ninh twenty some miles. Try to get that to my Poppa Lima (Platoon Leader). Over."

"Roger, One-Two, will relay to family, over."

"Yeah, roger that. I'm sure White is looking for me. One-Two out."

"It's a wonder anybody heard us," I said, as I turned off the FM, the UHF, and the ADF radios. I also turned off the anti-collision light and confirmed that I had turned off the navigation lights earlier.

"Well, that ought to do it," I said, more or less to myself but over the intercom. "We'll be to Loc Ninh in a few minutes."

I pulled out my cigarettes from my left shirt pocket. Our Troop A, 1/9th unit patch was sewn on the right pocket: a blue field with a yellow triangle on crossed sabers.

I looked over at Kiser after I managed to light my cigarette. He was staring out the left door, looking out at the jungle, his M-16 cradled in his arms.

"Robert, you alright?" I asked. "Robert, you okay?

"What, oh, yeah."

"I thought I lost you there for awhile."

"No, I'm okay.

Specialist Four Robert Kiser was a very quiet sort of a guy. I did not know much about him, other than he was from Pennsylvania. He had been flying with me for a couple months now, but he stayed very much to himself and almost never spoke. He was young, maybe 18 or 19, and thin. He had come to Apache from an infantry unit, after he had extended his tour for six months.

A lot of enlisted men and some officers had taken the offer of a six month extension on their tour in Vietnam, for a six month drop off of their enlistment. I could never understand why anyone would want to do that. I guess they just hated the thought of the stateside spit-shine army so much that they were willing to exchange an additional six months in Vietnam for a six month early out. A guy coming to the end of his twelve month tour, who had roughly a year to go in the Army, could extend an extra six months in Vietnam and go home a civilian.

I suppose I would understand someone who never saw danger doing that, but for our door gunners and observers, it seemed insane to me. I did not plan to spend one extra day in this country. If I survived this tour, I would spend whatever time I had to at any stateside assignment they gave me. *If* I survived this tour.

Kiser seemed to like Scouts -- at least I never heard him say anything against it. But then I never heard him say much about anything.

Sergeant Curtis Smoot was another story. We had flown together for several months now.

He was a Negro from somewhere in Louisiana. Smoot was outgoing, cheerful, and always in a good humor. He always tried to please. It bothered him to no end that he could not get his M-60 to fire correctly, not only because he knew that it was dangerous for us, but also because he was very conscientious about his job and the aircraft. That is probably why I liked him so much.

There was a lot of "black power" going on in Vietnam then, secret handshakes and all that, but Smoot was not in to that stuff. He hung around more with the guys in the Scout Platoon than he did with the "brothers."

I was closer to Smoot than I was to Kiser. I had known him longer, and he and I would often talk. He had told me once that the only letter he had ever gotten from his sister while he had been in Vietnam was to ask for money for a radio. You could tell he was still upset about it. *I* was upset about it. There was Curtis putting his life on the line every day, and she has the nerve to ask him for money for a radio. I wondered if his sister and his family had any idea what he was doing over here. I wondered if *anybody's* family had any idea what we were doing over here.

I really liked both Smoot and Kiser. The three of us worked well together. Aircrews in Vietnam were tight, and Scout crews were really tight. We were family. In the air we were no longer three separate people; we were a team. We knew what each other was thinking before we said it. We knew what each other was doing or about to do, without looking. The three of us operated as a machine. The more we flew together, the better the machine worked. We felt comfortable together, each of trusting the other to do his job the best way that he knew how. Rank, and position dictated that the major share of the responsibility fell in my lap. I was the pilot and I was in command. However, I was well aware that I was young. We discussed all important decisions among the three of us, and then we came to a consensus. That is....if we had time.

Kiser's job as Oscar, or observer, was to sit in the left front seat with his M-16 cradled in his arms, barrel pointed outside, and a red smoke grenade firmly held in both hands with the pin already pulled. The purpose of the red smoke was to mark the target, or actually *our* position when we took fire. From the red smoke I could then direct the Cobra as to where the fire was coming from. Often it was right underneath us, but sometimes it wasn't. Important that the observer did not forget to throw out the grenade. Often in the excitement of being fired upon, a new observer would forget to throw out the smoke, which meant that we had to go back in to toss the smoke while we, of course, took still more fire.

The term "observer" was misleading in that the truth was, the observer could see very little during the actual mission. In order for me, sitting in the right front seat, to see and have about the same field of vision as my Torque/Door Gunner, who sat directly behind me on the right side of the cargo floor, I flew in a tight right hand circle, nose high, nose to the left, out of trim, with the right side low so that my gunner and I could see. That meant the observer could not see at all, or very little, and with the heat, the aircraft circling and sometimes jerking with quick up and down movements, he often got airsick. It could not be helped; it was more important that the pilot and the gunner could see.

Configurations varied among Scout Platoons even in the same squadron. Some units liked to use the XM-27 minigun system, which fired 7.62 mm, the same as an M-60. Mounted on the left side and fired by the pilot, it put out a tremendous amount of fire power, usually set to fire 2000 rounds per minute. But because of the weight of the gun system, you had to give up a crewmember (usually the observer), which meant you had to give up another set of eyes. And it also meant, if you went down (and if you were flying Scouts, you were probably going to get shot down), you gave up having another person with another gun while you were waiting on the ground to be picked up. The XM-27 was heavy, electrically operated, and hard-mounted to the aircraft. It was now useless on the ground.

Our CO, Maj. Harris, was the only one in our troop who ever used it. He would go off on Scout missions with just his gunner Sgt. John Rice. Rice was one of the most experienced Torques we had and a great set of eyes.

The Door Gunner's job seems obvious, but besides being able to accurately handle and fire his 7.62 mm M-60 machine gun, he needed sharp eyes and common sense. Some Torques sat on the foldable nylon seat fastened to the engine bulkhead, but many preferred to sit on the cargo bay floor with their legs and feet hanging out. They wore a "monkey strap" fastened to the cargo floor so they could put their feet on the skids and hang forward out of the aircraft. This allowed them to see much more and to fire under the skids and below the tail boom of the ship. The M-60 was hand held and fired left-handed. It was not solidly mounted on a pintle (a metal post) hard mounted to the aircraft as many M-60's were on Hueys.

Some of our gunners liked to use the M-79 40 mm grenade launcher. It reminded me of a sawed off shotgun with a very large gauge. It was good for a lot of things, and we carried an assortment of grenades for it. It was used to fire an HE (high explosive) fragmentation grenade from it when you could not hit the target with a conventional hand thrown grenade. We also carried 40 mm smoke, “stink”, and “shotgun” shells. “Stink,” grenades were sometimes used on a rice cache that we were not able to destroy. After a couple of rounds of that stink gas, there would be no way that the enemy would be able to eat the rice.

Chapter Four

Loch Ninh was a small village on Highway 13 about ten kilometers south of the Cambodian border. A small rubber plantation formed an arc around the western edge of the village. Bordering the southwest side of the rubber plantation lay a single north-south runway that we were using as a staging area. This was where we launched our missions into Cambodia every day.

The runway had been built by the Frenchman who owned the rubber plantation. He flew in occasionally in his own plane to check on things. However, he lived in Saigon or somewhere down south. The plantation home, an old French stucco, sat on a hill about a mile north of the airstrip.

Sometimes I felt as if these bastards were the real reason why we were here. This guy, like the rest of the absentee plantation owners, was a holdover from the old French colonial days. Most of the really wealthy people in Vietnam were not Vietnamese; they were French or Chinese. They would not be able to hold on to their land if the communists ever took over, yet anytime we accidently destroyed their rubber groves, the United States Government was expected to pay for the damages. We had strict orders to avoid fighting battles in the rubber plantations.

The VC and the NVA loved to hide in the rubber. Like the jungle, the tops of the rubber trees blossomed out with limbs overlapping each other and hid everything beneath their canopy of leaves. However, unlike the jungle, the groves were planted in nice neat straight rows of trees, similar to an apple orchid, with access roads in between the rows. This made the large rubber plantations perfect for moving men and equipment without being seen from the air. Unless, of course, the people looking for them flew low and slow and hovered right down in the tops of the trees like we did.

Loc Ninh did not have a control tower; instead there was a common advisory frequency on FM. I made a call "in the blind" and turned on final (approach) for landing to the north. The "Headhunters," our Apache Troop Lift Platoon Hueys, were lined up along the east side of the runway facing north. It looked like most of the Pink Teams were already out on missions.

Our pilots and crews who were not flying, along with our "Blues," were just inside the tree line of the rubber, taking advantage of the shade. I knew they would be sleeping or playing cards. And, of course, there would be the ARVN "Browns," since we were not allowed to take our own Blues into Cambodia with us. In the event of a downed aircraft, we would have to rely on the Browns, transported and inserted by our own Hueys, to come in and get us out.

I used to watch them gather around us as we played cards at Loc Ninh. They seemed to be amazed by us. We were the Americans -- the white giants from the land of plenty, here to save them from the communists. We bewildered them. I am sure they thought we did everything in excess. We spent money in excess; we drank in excess; we screwed in excess. And from the look on their faces as they looked at American girlie magazines, American women had breasts in excess.

I often wondered, since this war was the only real contact that they had had with our culture, if the Vietnamese thought that all Americans sat at home with a whore in their lap, looking at *Playboy* magazines and drinking themselves into a stupor. That is what they saw us doing most of time in our hootches and in their bars and whorehouses. They damn sure did not see us fighting *their* enemy because they were never around when that was going on. Ah, but who's bitter?

I hovered over next to another LOH, set down, and began my shutdown procedure. The rotor blades had not stopped turning as White approached the aircraft. I could tell he was pissed. He did not like warrant officers in general, and he especially did not like me and my best friend Bob Spencer.

"Where in the hell have you been?" shouted Cpt. Daniel "Ace" Miller above the sound of the rotors winding down as he stuck his face in my door and in my face.

I took off my helmet and wiped the sweat from my forehead.

"Didn't you get the word that I had a broken aircraft?"

"Yeah, I heard, a generator, but what took you so fucking long to get here?"

"No, this one's got the bad generator! This is the second aircraft I've had this morning. I had a chip light in two-seven-three, so I had to get another aircraft and preflight all over again!"

"Well, you've got the next mission mister; I just flew the last two!"

"What happened to One-Six (WO1 Bob Smith)?" I asked.

"He's got engine problems."

"Well, what the hell am I gonna fly then?"

"You'll have to fly mine. Get your stuff transferred over to four-one-two; you'll be flying with Two-Five. I want you in the air in five minutes. You got that, Houser, five minutes!"

"Yes, sir, I got that," I said, as White stomped away. What a prick. There was no way in hell that I could be in the air in "five" minutes and he knew that.

"You get all that, Smoot?" I asked.

"Yeah, Mr. Houser. I got the idea. He doesn't like you much, does he?"

"Not much. Make sure you got what you want in those frag boxes. In fact, just switch our ammo boxes with four-one-two. I hate this. Every time I have to do this I leave something I need in the other aircraft. We will all check each other's stuff to make sure that doesn't happen."

"O.K, Mr. Houser."

"Kiser, help Smoot switch everything out, and make sure that you have exactly what you want in there, too. Don't forget your red smokes in the door."

"O.K., Mr. Houser", Kiser nodded as he grabbed the rope handles of one of our two ammo boxes. Smoot had already picked up the other one and was headed for 412, which, of course, was parked quite a distance from where we had shutdown.

We would have to move all of our personal equipment over to the other aircraft. We would also need to swap our ammo boxes. We carried two wooden ammo boxes. One was filled with 2200 rounds of 7.62 mm for Smoot's M-60. The other was filled with an assortment of hand grenades and sometimes homemade bombs (that we were not allowed to have). Each door gunner seemed to have his own preference as to how he packed his "frag" box and what he packed it with.

Some Torques liked a lot of fragmentary grenades and no concussion grenades at all. Others liked to carry a lot of incendiary grenades, which were good for burning and melting things; but they did not throw shrapnel. "Willie Petes," white phosphorus grenades, were a good combination because they would explode and splatter. The phosphorus would burn practically anything. They were particularly good for concealed hootches and structures that were hard to hit with an incendiary.

"Hey, Mr. Houser, do I have time to take a leak?" Smoot asked.

"Yes, Curtis, absolutely, go ahead."

"Well, I heard what Cpt. Miller said about us being in the air in five minutes."

"Yeah, I know, but it's not gonna happen. Go ahead and take a leak. In fact, I need to get rid of some coffee, too. Kiser, do you need to use the shitter?"

"No, I'm okay." he said.

"You sure? I don't know where it is, but now's the time to use it if you need to," I yelled, as I walked over towards Smoot who was already watering a rubber tree.

It did not look as if we had missed much that morning. The activity was much the same since we started using Loc Ninh as a staging area. A couple of crew chiefs were working on a Huey, but all the rest of our people were in the shade of the rubber trees. Our guys lounged and slept in plastic hammocks stretched between the trees all around the area. Others were tied inside Huey cargo bays, suspended from the crew seat upright posts to the back of the pilot's seats.

There were several games of Poker and Spades being played on blankets laid out on the ground that had been brought along for that purpose.

Our presence here was great for the local economy; all of the town's vendors were out in force peddling whatever they had to sell. The amazing thing was that they were here waiting on us early in the morning of the first day of the "secret" invasion.

The villagers were selling a local form of soda pop and banana-flavored popsicles. Others were selling hammocks and plastic mats to lie on. And, as always, the town whores were working their way through the troop area trying to drum up business. They would take their customers farther back into the rubber trees or on into the village. Looked like business was good.

Scattered around the area in small groups watching our people play cards were the ARVNs, the company of South Vietnamese Browns attached to us. We knew we would lose aircraft in Cambodia, probably several. The probability was very high that we would also lose lives when those aircraft went down. These were the guys that were supposed to find us and rescue us. None of us had much faith that when the time came they would be ready or willing to do their jobs.

Watching them here at Loc Ninh every day, I realized that they seemed to be the quintessential reason why South Vietnam would never win the war. There probably was not anyone in this group over 18 or 19 years old. I was sure they were all draftees. None of them appeared to have any combat experience. We could usually tell. None of these guys even looked as if they would ever be capable of surviving a firefight. Unlike most of us, they all looked as if they would be more than happy to spend every day here under the rubber trees at Loc Ninh.

They sat, or they squatted, or slept, and all the while they studied us suspiciously. They seemed to be fascinated by us. But it was always a guarded fascination. They did not look upon us as "allies," but always with apprehension and always with distrust. I assumed that this was another legacy of their long-time relationship with the French. We were as strange and offensive to them as they were to us.

I respected the Vietcong and the North Vietnamese even more, but I had no feeling or compassion for the South Vietnamese which we were here to defend. I had come to Vietnam naively thinking that we were here to save these "brave" people and their "noble" government in Saigon from the communists who wanted to take over the world. But that was an eternity ago, and my views on the war and the reasons for it had changed greatly as the months had passed.

I now accepted the fact that President Thieu's regime in Saigon was not the noble government that Americans had been led to believe. It was instead a government of corruption, a dictatorship just as oppressive as the one that we were here to defend it from.

It was not difficult to see why these young South Vietnamese soldiers had eventually become disinterested in the war. They, and their fathers before them, had fought for years in the army of one dictatorship or another. It did not matter whether the communists won or whether this year's government in Saigon won, these people would never have any real political freedoms. All they wanted was for the war to be over. I was not sure if the majority of them even cared who won anymore.

That was the thing that disturbed me the most. They did not seem to care about fighting the war and winning it. And if *they* did not care about fighting the war and winning it, then what the hell were *we* doing here? Why, for example, were American boys being drafted to fight in this war, when wealthy politically connected Vietnamese families could buy their kids way out of the Vietnamese draft and send them to American universities where they were safe? That just did not make any sense to me. The gravity of these questions was very sobering, and I found myself asking them more and more lately.

None of this changed the way I flew my missions or did my job. I had volunteered for Scouts and I was going to stay in Scouts. I still did the very best job that I could do every day. However, the ultimate mission to defeat the communist and protect the government in Saigon was no longer my personal mission. My personal mission was now basic survival, for me, and for the men who flew with me, and for the other men of Apache Troop. I would do my best just like always to find and kill the "bad guys," But the most important mission I had was to keep the men of Apache Troop alive, especially my crew.

As I walked over to 412, I passed by three ARVNs sitting a few feet behind the drainage ditch that ran next to the runway. Two ponchos tied together with sticks formed a lean-to device for shade. A pot of rice was heating on a small fire in front of them. They paid no attention to me walking by because they were totally engrossed in a *Playboy* that they had somehow stolen or traded for. They sat and giggled like little boys as they eagerly turned the pages, oblivious to me, to the war, to their rice, and to the fact that their M-16s were lying in the dirt. One rifle had slipped, muzzle first, all the way down the embankment of the ditch. An NVA soldier would have been shot or beaten for that. Of course, an NVA soldier would know the value of the weapon because he would intend to use it.

I did an abbreviated pre-flight, looking at what I had learned were the very most important things to check, and a few minutes later we were cranked and ready to hover out. Smoot and Kiser had switched our ammo boxes and equipment over to 412, and we seemed to be all set.

"Hey, One-Two, …you up uniform yet, …this is Two-Five?"

Foti and Osborn were already cranked and waiting.

"Roger, Two-Five, this is One-Two, I'm about ready."

"O.K., One-Two, if you'll follow us out of here we'll be departing north. We're gonna go ahead and take off. Over."

"Roger, Two-Five, I'll be with you in a minute."

As I lifted 412 into a six-inch hover, I noticed the three ARVNs still looking at the *Playboy* magazine. I could not resist. I hovered on over to the drainage ditch and watched as the rotor wash engulfed the three gigglers in a swirling tornado of dust and dirt. Everything blew away, ponchos, rice, the *Playboy*, -- everything. One of the gooks was chasing the disintegrating magazine down the ditch, while another tried to recover the ponchos. I loved it.

"Hey, Mr. Houser, what are you trying to do?" asked Smoot.

"Win the hearts and minds, Curtis. Win the hearts and minds."

As I started to hover away, one of the more indignant soldiers, who had been shaking his fist at us and giving us the "finger," began to search in the dust for his rifle. Smoot saw this too, and the two of us must have been thinking the same thing. I peddle turned the nose of the aircraft to the left and put the guy right in front of Smoot's right side cargo door. He rotated his M-60 out of the door and locked in a fresh belt of ammo. The ARVN decided that our M-60 "trumped" his M-16 and that it was safer to shake his fist than to grab his gun. Smoot kept his M-60 trained on the guy just in case he changed his mind. We did a clearing turn, I made a radio call advising that we were taking off to the north, and we hovered out to the runway. I eased 412 forward through translational lift, and we were on the go. Another exciting day at Loc Ninh.

"Curtis, did I ever tell you how much I love ya?"

"What did you say, Mr. Houser?"

"Never mind."

Chapter Five

We caught up with 25 two or three miles north of Loc Ninh. It was about 13:30 (1:30), and by now even at two thousand feet it was very hot. The jungle had changed to scattered trees with large open areas. We continued to follow Highway 13 as it ran generally northwest out of Loc Ninh towards Snuol. Somewhere below us was the border. It was about fifteen klicks (kilometers) from Loc Ninh to the border and about the same from the border to Snuol. There was no river in this area defining the border, and there were no markers that we could see from this altitude, but we were now in Cambodia.

Snuol was still out of sight to the northwest, but we could begin to see the rubber plantation that surrounded it on the north and west. This was the Chup Rubber Plantation, and it was much larger than the plantation at Loc Ninh. Some days earlier, we had been involved in what had turned out to be a large battle between the ARVNs and an NVA unit. Almost the entire battle was fought in the rubber, which made it difficult for us to lend close air support with our Cobras or with air strikes from jet fighter bombers because of the visibility problem. Only a Scout bird could fly low enough and slow enough to make out anything in the rubber trees.

"One-Two, this is Two-Five, how do you hear?" There was no mistaking Paul Foti's New York accent.

"I have you Lima Chuck, how me?" I answered.

"I have you loud and clear also. O.K., what we're gonna do here, is you follow me up the highway here, and we're going up north of Snuol and look around up there north of the river, so we're really looking for that."

"Copy" I answered.

"Hey, …and uh, One-Two."

"Yeah."

"I still got your body bag, baby,…maybe today's the day."

"Yeah, and you know where you can shove that body bag, too, don't you, asshole?"

"You mean he carries a body bag just for you?" Smoot asked, "I thought that only the Hueys carried those."

"Oh, he's been telling me that ever since he was a Huey driver. When I first met him and he found out I had volunteered for Scouts, he told me how stupid I was. Then he started telling me that he was carrying a body bag on his aircraft, just for me. That shit gets old after awhile."

"Yeah, man, I didn't like that part about 'maybe today's the day'! That's cold man! Wow!"

Snuol was below us now, passing out the left door. The village was on the southeast side of the rubber plantation. On the extreme southeast side of the village was a small compound in the middle of a large dried-up rice field. That compound was what we really referred to as Snuol. That was the headquarters of the ARVN division we were supporting.

The compound was about a mile west of Highway 13 and did not sit on any of the main (dirt) roads. Like most ARVN compounds, it was built partially underground, and what was above ground was covered with sandbags and dirt. Bunkers and concertina barbed wire surrounded the main buildings. A landing pad sat on the south side of the complex just outside the wire. The entire perimeter was surrounded by a minefield.

A couple of times a day the ARVNs would request one of our Hueys to come in and pick up some Vietnamese general or VIP or drop somebody off. None of our pilots liked to land there because every time they did the place got mortared.

I was generally familiar with the area surrounding Snuol and the rubber, at least from the air. I had never been on the ground there, but the farther north that we flew, the less I had seen. Today we would be working north of the river in an area I had *never* worked or seen. In fact, none of Apache Troop had been as far north as we would be working today.

I tried to get an idea of the lay of the land as we flew. The road continued to run generally north slowly bending from time to time. The sparse trees and clearings became thicker forests with fewer open areas. Highway 13, if that is still what they called it here, was the only major road in the area. It was a "hardstand" road, but it was barely two lanes wide, and it certainly did not represent what we considered a "highway" back in the States. If we had followed it south out of Loc Ninh, it would have taken us to An Loc and eventually all the way to Saigon, the way I wished we were going. I did not know where it was taking us to the north, but it could not be anywhere good.

After a few more minutes of flying, I saw a single Huey orbiting high over the river. It was our Command and Control ship. In Vietnam the Cobra always ran our Pink team missions, but since we had been operating in Cambodia, we had the luxury of C & C birds. While the Scout was working low-level, and the Cobra covered him from about two thousand feet, the C & C bird sat up at about four thousand and circled around directing the entire mission.

He was nice to have around for several reasons, but the most important one for us was that if we got shot down, he could come down and try to pick us up. There had been Scouts picked up by Cobras, but they had had to ride the rocket pods out. The tiny cockpit on the Snake only held the two pilots one behind the other. There was no room for any passengers. The thought of hopping on a rocked pod facing backwards and lying over the stub wing did not appeal much to me. Needless to say, in that situation I would take it.

We "married up" with the Huey and crossed the river where Highway 13 intersected it. Below was an old two-span iron bridge, which had been partially blown up some years before. The northern span, disconnected from the center support, lay crumpled in the river partially submerged. Its rusted hulk was still connected to the north bank. The other span did not appear to be badly damaged, but the bridge was, of course, unusable.

The road turned west just north of the river, and we turned with it. The vegetation had gotten very thick and had become triple canopy jungle. I was still at altitude slightly lower and just to the left and behind 25. We began to fly over an area of foothills. The road was still visible, and from time to time we could see portions of other hard-packed dirt roads that joined it. It was hard to tell from this altitude where they went or if they had any common direction.

We continued further west. I had a very uneasy feeling about this. My discomfort was a combination of things: my usual nervous stomach; we were farther north than we had ever worked and not familiar with this area; the closest "friendlies" were at least twenty-five klicks to the south, and they were ARVNs; and that business that morning about breaking two aircraft and now flying a third. That all made me feel as though maybe we were not supposed to fly today.

Well, shit, shake it off. I had never turned down a mission yet, and I was not going to start now. My stomach had been upset every mission that I had flown in Cambodia, so that was nothing new. I did wish that I was flying my own 273, the bird that I was most familiar and comfortable with.

"One-Two, Two-Five, you ready to go down?"

"Yeah, roger that, how about a test fire?" I asked.

"Just a minute," Foti responded.

"O.K., you guys ready to go?" I asked. "Smoot, you ready?"

"Yes, sir, I'm ready," Smoot said, as he rearranged his M-60 and edged out further into the doorway.

Kiser reached over and grabbed a red smoke grenade from a wire loop at the door hinge, pulled the pin, and held the spoon down with his left thumb. He held the grenade close to his body in his left hand and draped his M-16 across his lap with his right.

"One-Two, you're clear to fire," Foti said.

"Roger that, I'm going hot," I said, then shifted my thumb to the other side of the mike button so that I would be speaking only inside the aircraft, "Smoot, you're clear to fire your sixty."

Ba-ba-ba-ba-ba-ba-ba-ba,...Ba-ba-ba-ba-ba-ba-ba. Smoot cut loose with two short bursts of his M-60. No jam.

"It's okay, Mr. Houser."

"Yeah, well, we'll see," I said. I was not convinced. It always worked on the first test fire.

"Two-Five, we're ready to go down," I said.

"Yeah, go ahead, One-Two. This area is fine," replied Foti.

I pushed in right pedal, lowered the collective pitch, and slipped into a tight right-hand spiraling descent. I was looking straight at the ground over my right shoulder. In seconds we had dropped through over 1500 feet of stifling hot air, and we were now at the tops of the trees. The technique was meant to descend as quickly as possible through the "dead man zone" (50 to 1500 feet) and thereby present a target for the shortest time as possible, another maneuver not taught in flight school. I kept my airspeed up at about eighty knots. None of that ten or fifteen knot flying like we did on the mission in Vietnam. These bastards over here were too good for that.

My tight right hand circles were larger than normal because of the increased airspeed.

We still had one or two "old" Scout pilots who were here during the first Cambodian incursion back in May and June of 1970, and they had warned us what to expect. They were adamant that we could not conduct Scout missions the way we were used to. No hovering over a suspected area. No overflying a clearing. Stay in the tree line. No low airspeeds.

I looked at my watch; my left nomex glove was rolled up so that it was visible. It was almost two o'clock. I figured I would have roughly an hour "on station," leaving myself enough fuel for a 25 or 30 minute flight back to Loc Ninh.

"OK, One-two, I'd like you to work these foothills from here to the north and west. Over," said Foti.

"Roger that, I've got numerous trails and roads everywhere. Stand by."

"OK, we're ready to copy."

"Roger, I've got a southeast-northwest road, six to eight feet wide, moderate to heavy use last twelve to twenty-four hours. It's had a lot of shit down it, and recently. It runs on the north side and about parallel with the highway and.....OK, just a minute...yeah, OK, it junctions with the highway down here in at least two places. It doesn't appear to cross it, though."

"OK, what's it had on it?"

"I can't really tell, but a lot of something. I haven't seen any tracked vehicle marks so far. The road is dry and packed down hard, can't tell the direction of travel yet."

"OK," Foti replied.

"I've got another north-south road, six-to-eight-feet wide, moderate to heavy use last twelve to two-four hours. Another road generally east-west this time, six-to-eight-feet wide, moderate to heavy use last twelve to two-four. You're gonna run out of grease pencil and canopy!" I said excitedly.

In the Cobra, the AC (aircraft commander) sat in the back seat and flew while the copilot sat in the front and operated the chin turret. He also acted as secretary. Every bit of information that he received from the "low-bird" was written down in a sort of shorthand with a grease pencil on the Plexiglas canopy. Then later, on the way home from the mission, he would relay the information back to flight operations.

"I have numerous fighting positions everywhere. They're about three-by-five feet and three feet deep. A few bunkers around the area, probably eight-by-ten, heavy overhead cover."

"How many fighting positions and bunkers?" Foti asked.

"Oh, shit, maybe thirty fighting positions this general area, maybe five to eight bunkers."

"Roger," Foti replied.

I also had been doing this long enough to know that fighting positions and bunkers were like mice: for every one that you could see, there were several more that you did not see. Nevertheless, I was reporting what I actually saw. Someone at a higher level in division G2 (intelligence) would interpret all these reports, combine them with other Scout reports from us and other units doing the same thing and eventually come up with a "big picture" idea of what was really going on.

"I have numerous trails running everywhere. Most 6 to12 inches, some 12 to 24 inches wide, moderate to heavy use last twelve to two-four hours. I think most of what we're seeing here is foot traffic. I don't see anything to indicate bicycles. I still can't tell the direction."

"OK, One-Two, move your circles so that you follow that one road to the northwest," Foti advised.

"Roger that. These fighting positions and bunkers have been here awhile, but this traffic is recent…very recent," I said.

It was difficult in the dry season to figure the direction of travel. I assumed it was generally south, but I wanted to find something to confirm that. The ground was not soft enough to pick up on footprints or tire tracks, and yet I did not see any dust. A lot of dust would have indicated very heavy use and also helped me with footprints.

I was also looking for tramped-down grass next to the narrow trails. Bicycles were heavily laden with supplies and not ridden but pushed by someone walking next to them so that the bicycle was on the trail, not the person.

I began to change my right hand circles so that my overall movement was northwest. We followed the road for a few more minutes until it intersected one running north. We followed that one for two or three miles. Everywhere we looked there was more of the same: roads, trails, fighting positions, bunkers; a lot of people had been through this area in the last few days. But which way were they traveling, and where were they now? We continued to work the same area for several more minutes.

"OK, One-Two, break to the northeast here. I want to bring you up to altitude and move you," Foti instructed.

"Roger, Two-Five."

"Look sharp, you guys, we're coming up," I warned Kiser and Smoot.

I started a climb to the northeast. This was a critical time in this type of flying, too high to use the tops of the trees for concealment but too low to be out of range of small arms fire. Fortunately, we did not take any fire. I leveled off at 2000 feet (indicated altitude) and flew northeast for a few minutes. I did not recognize anything; it is easy to get disoriented when you are low level and cannot see any landmarks. We were still over foothills. I was not able to see the river or Highway 13; they had to be farther south. I wanted to see one or the other, preferably both to get my bearings. No luck.

"OK, One-Two, I'm going to put you down right here."

"Roger that," I answered.

It was about 14:30 (2:30); we had been cranked a little over an hour. We had another 25 or 30 minutes left on station. It seemed as though we had been here forever. I was soaked with sweat.

This area was very much the same as the others: more trails, fighting positions, and bunkers. The fighting positions and bunkers all seemed to be old and I did not see any sign of recent use. But, needless to say, they were already there if the NVA needed them.

"I have a southeast-northwest trail, 12 to 24 inches, moderate to heavy use, last twelve to two-four hours. Make that heavy use," I told Foti.

"O.K., One-Two, I want you to move more to the southeast now..."

"Wait a minute, I want to work this trail a little longer," I said.

"What do you have?"

"I don't know yet...numerous fighting positions, three-by-five-feet deep. A few bunkers, eight-by-ten heavy overhead cover. I have a 12 to 24 inch trail coming from the east intersecting the trail I'm on now. Moderate to heavy use last twelve to two-four hours. I'm gonna stay with the first one. Something's down here."

"What do you have?" Foti asked.

"I don't know. It just doesn't look right," I replied.

This trail was different from the others that we had looked at. There was something about this one. I was not sure yet what it was. There was something different. I was getting excited.

"Curtis, what's wrong with this?" I asked Smoot.

"What do you mean, Mr. Houser?" Smoot asked.

"I mean something is different about this trail!"

"I don't know, Mr. Houser. I don't like any of it," Smoot said hesitantly.

"What have you got, One-Two?" Foti was getting impatient.

"More fighting positions, more bunkers, another trail coming in from the east. There's dust on this trail, and its getting wider! This son-of-a-bitch has had heavy use, and I mean lately!"

The trail curved more to the east. I saw something on that last pass just to the side of the trail, something out of place.

"Curtis, did you see that?" I asked.

"What?"

"I'm not sure yet, just off the side of the trail. I'm coming back around."

"Two-Five, I've got something down here just off the side of the trail. Now where the hell was that?" I said to Smoot.

"I got it, Mr. Houser, come right, come right!" Now Smoot was excited.

As the thick bamboo parted with the rotor wash, it exposed a pile of sticks, but they were not sticks. Everything was always larger on the ground than it appeared from the air. It was freshly cut bamboo, a whole pile of it!

"Two-Five, I've got a pile of freshly cut bamboo! It's cut in four-to-six-foot lengths. This shit is new, brand new! So are these bunkers. My God, they're all over the place and they haven't been here long! These are not like the ones that we have been looking at; these are brand new! They're gonna use this bamboo to build something, and they don't like to carry that shit very far!"

"O.K., One-Two, watch yourself."

"They're here. I know they're here somewhere, I can feel it. They're watching us right now!"

"I got something over here, Mr. Houser!" yelled Smoot. Now he was really excited.

"Two-Five, we've got another pile of bamboo down here. The underbrush in this whole area is trampled down!"

"Spider hole!" yelled Smoot.

"OK, we've got a fresh spider hole, with about a one-by-one-foot entrance! It's brand new! Hell, I'll bet it wasn't here two days ago! There's another one…there's two more! They're all around here!" I yelled to Foti.

"I got them over here too!" said Kiser.

"Smoot, you and Kiser stay alert now. I know they're here somewhere!" I said loudly over the intercom.

Kiser was still clutching his smoke grenade, ready to throw it out as soon as we took fire. I could not see Smoot, since he sat directly behind me, but I knew he was getting anxious too. They should have shot at us by now. What were they waiting for? They always heard us and then saw us before we saw them. That was the nature of Scouts. We were bait.

The trail wound around a small hill and suddenly opened into a clearing. There in the middle of the clearing, looking like an ant hill, was a bunker under construction.

"Holy shit, I've got a brand new bunker down here! It's still under construction! It's more like an underground building! Very heavy overhead cover, walk down entrance with steps! Looks like the roof must be supported with logs! They've got boards and bamboo lying all over the place! We must have caught them by surprise!"

"Watch your ass, One-Two!" yelled Foti.

"Look sharp now, you guys!" I warned Kiser and Smoot.

The whole area is trampled down, three-by-five fighting positions everywhere, new ones! We're gonna recon by fire!"

"Roger, be careful," said Foti.

"Smoot, start shooting up that tree line around the clearing. Kiser, watch your side. Be sharp," I warned.

Ba-ba-ba-ba-ba-ba-ba...Ba-ba-ba-ba-ba-ba...Ba-ba-ba-ba-ba-ba-ba-ba, Smoot started ripping into the tree line.

"We've got a lot of brand new three-by-five fighting positions just inside the tree line of this clearing. Spider holes all around," I told Foti.

Ba-ba-ba-ba-ba-ba-ba...Ba-ba-ba-ba-ba-ba-ba-ba.

"O.K., hold your fire and get a frag ready," I yelled to Smoot.

Reconning by fire with the M-60 often made the gooks think that they had been spotted. The hope was that they would then return fire, giving away their position, thinking that we already knew where they were and could see them. Of course, it did not always work. The more experienced NVA and VC knew what we were doing and did not take the bait.

"You got that frag ready?" I asked Smoot.

"Yeah, I'm ready!" Smoot yelled, as he held a fragmentation grenade out his right cargo door.

I headed for the entrance to the bunker. Fifty meters from the entrance I pulled the nose back and flared the aircraft to slow the airspeed.

"Ready…drop!" I said as I pulled in power and dumped the nose over to gain airspeed and get clear. I turned my head around in time to watch the frag hit next to the entrance and roll down the outside of the bunker. "Ka-boom!"

"Fuck, we missed…get another grenade!" I yelled into the mike.

Hitting an opening from the air with a grenade was a real challenge. Even with this comparatively large opening, the timing had to be exact. We had done this many times, but it was still hard to do. The best way was to come to a stationary hover and drop it in the hole, and we often did that in Vietnam, but I was not going to do that here. I slowed down to about ten knots. We made a wide right hand turn low over the bamboo, and now we were coming up on the edge of the clearing again.

"OK, here we go again," I said mainly to Smoot. "Eyes sharp, everybody!"

I lined up with the entrance for the second time, fully expecting a figure to pop out of the opening and start blasting away with his AK. We would be most vulnerable during that flare in front of the bunker, suspended in midair a few feet above the entrance, with no airspeed, no altitude, and no concealment.

"Ready……drop!"

I was sure that we hit it that time. I knew, of course, that we could not hurt the bunker, but we damn sure could hurt whoever might be hiding inside. We could also get lucky and have this bunker turn out to be where they were storing their ammo or fuel.

"It went right in this time, Mr. Houser!" yelled Smoot, half hanging out of the door so that he could look behind and under us.

I could tell from the fuzzy static noise on the intercom that he was out in the slipstream; the air was blowing over his mike boom on his helmet, and it was hard to hear him.

Ka-boooom! This report was a much duller explosion than the first one, more of a rumble. We had rolled that one right down the steps. Smoke and dust poured out of the opening in a big cloud.

"That'll piss 'em off," I said.

Still no one shot at us, and no individuals were in sight. I knew damn well they were there below us somewhere close by, watching and waiting for the right moment. They knew how we worked our Pink Team missions; they knew there would be a gunship up above somewhere whether they saw him or not. Only the most inexperienced and foolhardy would shoot at us without an order to do so, thereby giving away their hiding place and drawing the wrath of the Cobra.

That was how smart these NVA "regulars" were. They knew if they fired on us we would drop everything in the inventory on top of them. They were smart enough to be willing to sacrifice a few soldiers and still not be suckered into giving away their position. They were close. They were very close.

"One-Two, we're getting down on time. I want you to break south. I have one more area I want you to look at before we leave. How is your fuel?" Foti asked.

I turned south and remained low level while I checked my fuel gauge and watch. In the excitement, time had passed very quickly. It was a few minutes after three.

"Roger. I can give you just a few more minutes," I said.

"OK, stay on that south heading, and I'll bring you up to altitude in just a minute," Foti advised.

"Roger that."

I tried to quickly recalculate my fuel burn rate so I would not cut myself short on the fuel that I would need to return to Loc Ninh. OH-6 fuel gauges were notoriously inaccurate. Most of us relied more on our watches than on the gauges.

"One-Two, go ahead and come up to altitude. I'm gonna put you down one more place. Over," said Foti.

"Roger, be advised, I only have ten minutes at the most to give you; don't cut me short," I said.

"Roger that."

I pulled in power with the collective and started to climb. We were holding 75 knots and headed generally south. We were probably 75 to 100 feet above the trees.

The initial explosion was not close by nor, was it particularly loud, but the concussion and shock of the impact that followed was crushing. The tiny aircraft jolted violently, as if a giant hand had struck it midair and shook it. I instinctively looked to the right and saw a small puff of smoke rising from the site of the launcher. I thought that we had been hit by a B-40 or an RPG (rocket propelled grenade). It had hit us on the right side, probably in the engine area, and we were on fire.

"I'm hit, I'm hit!" I yelled into the mike to Foti.

Events began to take place in hundredths or even thousandths of a second. I looked at the instrument panel; the Engine Out light was on. I heard the engine and transmission winding down in a low-pitched whine. I looked below us for an open area; there was nothing but jungle. Then to our front appeared a river running diagonally from left to right across our path. I thought that if I could hold enough collective pitch to keep us above the trees until we reached the river, I could then drop down into the "groove" in the top of the jungle canopy, turn right down the river, and hope that I had enough rotor RPM left for a flare a few feet above the water.

That would be the plan then. The river would save us. We would turn to the right down the river, avoiding the trees and the jungle, and make a flared "ditching" into the river. The water landing would also help us with the fire. My momentary relief was shattered when I found that I had no cyclic control. The cyclic (the "stick") controls the rotor system that the aircraft is suspended under. Whichever way the "disc" is pointed, the fuselage of the aircraft will follow.

The controls were stiff and would not respond; I no longer had control of the aircraft. We were now just along for the ride. I watched the river that I had hoped would save us pass under us. The jungle was quickly coming up to meet us. Without being able to turn down the river valley, we would overshoot the river and crash somewhere on the other side of it. I looked forward and down through the chin bubble and saw the tops of the trees of the opposite river bank zooming up at me. No longer were the branches and leaves far enough away that they appeared only as a mass of vegetation. In nano-seconds the trees had become branches, the branches had become clusters of leaves, and now I was quite literally counting the individual leaves on the branches. The tops of the trees rushed up to meet us…I knew we were dead.

Then time and motion were somehow suspended, and I had time to think about those things dearest to me, my family, my home, my friends. It was as though God had granted me one last opportunity to remember those things that mattered most to me in my life.

I did not think about death itself. I thought mainly about how my death would affect my family, mainly my mother and small brother. My mother was a very kind gentle person, and she would take my death very hard, as would the rest of the family. I thought about my dad and how he would take the news. My friends would miss me. I realized that the cliché about life "passing before your eyes" at the moment of death was truc. Whocvcr was thc vcry first guy to say that or writc that had obviously been himself about to die very suddenly. My life did pass before me. Maybe not my entire life, but I was able to think about much more, and in much greater detail than time should have allowed.

The aircraft crashed into the trees of the jungle somewhere above the riverbank and exploded on impact with the ground. The inertia of traveling almost ninety miles an hour hurled what remained of the OH-6A, 67-16412, into the river, and it sank to the bottom.

I was drowning! My mind raced to catch up with what had happened, but it could not.

Only seconds had passed since we had been hit with the RPG, and I had seen the tops of the trees racing up to kill us. I had known, and I had accepted that I was going to die in the crash, and now I was drowning! Everything was happening so quickly that my mind could not process all the information it was receiving. What was happening to me? Where was I? Why couldn't I breathe? My mind could not comprehend that I had somehow lived through the crash and now I was drowning on the bottom of the river!

I unsnapped my chinstrap and got my helmet off. I unfastened with one hand the "quick-release" feature of the combination seat belt shoulder harness restraint system. Both shoulder harnesses and the seat belt all came together and locked with one device in the center of my lap. All Army aircraft had that system just for this purpose. As the shoulder harness disconnected, the "chicken plate," or protective body armor that I had been wearing, fell off and away from me, as I had hoped it would.

Some months before I had started wearing body armor. A few of us had decided that if we ever went down in water, the weight of the protective vest and the difficulty to get out of it would probably drown us. After you put your head through the opening, there were two Velcro straps that wrapped around the front of the vest. The actual "plate" was not metal, but instead a piece of laminated ceramic form-fitted to the shape of a generic chest. There was another plate for your back, but no one ever wore it. Each plate fit into a large pocket also closed with Velcro flaps.

I had decided that all I really needed was the chest plate. I had taken it out of the vest and threw the vest away. The plate had a nylon strap at the top perfect for using as a handle to carry it back and forth to the aircraft. Every day I rested my chicken plate on my lap against my chest and positioned the shoulder harness straps over the plate to hold it in place as I fastened my belt.

It stayed in place fine and afforded me some protection and a sense of security. I realized, however, that if I took a direct hit with an armor piercing round, the plate would be of little use.

I heard bullets exploding behind me. The tremendous heat from the fire was causing the 7.62 mm M-60 ammunition in the cargo bay to "cook off," The random detonations shook whatever was left of 412. How could anything burn like that underwater? There must have been air trapped back there somehow and the fuel was feeding the fire.

I did not know how long I had been underwater. It seemed it had taken me an eternity to get out of my helmet and then the shoulder harness and belt. My lungs were screaming for oxygen. I finally climbed out of what I thought was still a doorway and started to swim to the surface. I do not even know how I knew where the surface was. I tried to kick my feet in combat boots and a flight suit. I could not see the surface. I thought, "My God, how deep am I?" My lungs were burning. It was the same feeling I'd had had as a kid trying to swim the length of the park pool underwater. I did not think that I was going to make it; my lungs were going to explode.

After what seemed like forever, I broke the surface of the water. Because I was so desperate for air I did not look above me first, as I had been trained, to see if was clear of fuel and fire. Thankfully it was, and the huge gasp of air that I took in although extremely hot was life-saving. I had somehow managed to surface just at the edge of the clear water that was not yet burning with fuel. Everything up river from me was burning with JP-4, and the advancing edge of that fire was almost to me.

My throat was scorched and burned. My lungs ached, and I could barely see; everything was fuzzy and out of focus. The relative silence that I had experienced underwater had now been replaced by the loud cracking and popping of AK-47s and .30 cal. machine guns. Everywhere the jungle was burning and at the same time alive with machine gun fire. It was difficult to distinguish between the sounds of the weapons firing and the crackling and popping of the jungle burning. There were tracers everywhere, but they did not seem to be coming at me; they seemed to all be going up into the air.

I tried to make my legs work to swim to the south riverbank. North Vietnamese soldiers were already running out of the jungle on the north bank, but they were all firing up apparently at the Cobra. I could not see Foti, but I could hear the distinctive sound of the gunship, and he was close. I reached the shore and started to drag myself up the riverbank, grabbing tree roots and grass for handholds. The bank was steep, and I kept sliding back down into the water. I was sure that I would be seen. I managed to reach the top of the bank and crawled into the nearby brush.

I pulled my Smith & Wesson revolver out of my shoulder holster. It looked awfully small. I wished that I had my M-16, which was now somewhere on the bottom of the river.

By now the NVA had begun to fire everything they had at the Cobra. I recognized not only the distinctive sound of AKs and .30 cal. machinegun fire, but also the heavy thump-thump-thump of at least one .51 cal. machinegun. I moved on into the brush another fifty meters or so and hid behind a large bush.

I was terrified, and I'm sure I was in shock. I could not believe that we had been shot down. I could not believe that I was here on the ground. My mind raced to catch up with the reality of the moment. Not the moment of five minutes ago --- that might as well have been ten years ago! I felt the bitter metallic taste of panic trying to take control. I fought it. Where were Kiser and Smoot? Did they make it out too? Why weren't they here? Why hadn't I seen them?

I ached all over; I was sore and stiff. My face and eyes were burning. I began to look myself over. I touched my face; it was bleeding and badly burned. I noticed that my new Seiko watch was missing. There was a two-inch wide flash burn on the top of my left wrist where I had rolled up my flight glove to be able to see my watch. That was a mistake and a bad habit. I was bleeding from a small cut on the bottom of the same wrist, apparently where the watch had been torn off.

As I surveyed the rest of my body, I suddenly realized that I was blind in my left eye. I touched it to see if it was still there. It was. I closed my right eye; I was getting some light through the left, but I could not see anything with it. Then I closed my left eye and checked the right one. I could see with it, but everything was fuzzy especially up close. I could not find any broken bones. I did not think to look to see if I had been shot.

I heard Foti and Osborn coming down the river low level. The sky was filled with AK-47 and .30 cal. machinegun tracers. The tracers zigzagged back and forth across the sky in the direction of the Cobra. I came out from my hiding place behind the large bush and waved my hands and arms while I jumped up and down.

Foti and Osborn were not firing yet. They had slowed their airspeed in order to look for us. They were close enough for me to see the pilot's helmeted heads in the canopy as they made a low slow pass over the crash site. I knew that they had not seen me, and I moved back behind the bushes. I thought about firing a pen flare but realized that even if they saw it, they would undoubtedly mistake it for another tracer (even though it was red and NVA and VC tracers are usually green) I left the flare gun in my holster.

Foti made another low and slow "dry" pass down the river. I again ran out from behind the bush, waved my arms wildly and jumped up and down. Again their aircraft was surrounded by tracers and again they did not see me. They were so close! Why couldn't they see me? I wanted to yell at them, "Hey I'm right here!" I had the sense to know that the only people that could possibly hear me yelling would be the "bad guys." I probably could not yell anyway; my throat was scorched and burned.

Foti continued to make low passes down the river. I thought each one was slower than the last one. With each pass, I came out from behind my bush, revealed myself, and jumped up and down waving my hands and arms. Each time they dodged tracers and trees, and each time they failed to see me. "Hey, guys, I'm right here! Please, I'm right here!" I knew, of course, what was happening; there was just too much to look at and too much to absorb for them to see me. I was sure they would also be shot down. They could not keep making those low slow passes and not get hit. I could not tell how fast Foti was flying, but I knew it was damn slow for a Cobra. Foti and Osborn made seven to ten passes altogether, and then I did not hear them anymore. I knew they had given us up.

The realization struck me that they were not going to see me or pick me up. Instead, in all probability, I would be killed or captured in the next few minutes right here, right behind this bush, on this river, in the middle of nowhere in Cambodia.

I looked at the .38 cal. revolver in my right hand. I did not intend to allow myself to be captured. I pulled the hammer back with my thumb cocking the weapon. I thought to myself, "So this is how it ends." I was not going to let the NVA capture me so they could torture me or keep me in a tiger cage buried in shit until I died. As long as I had the revolver, I still had the means to keep that from happening. But should I use it now? There was no other way out of this. They were probably all around me. It was going to be over in a matter of minutes, maybe seconds.

I realized they had probably figured out what had happened to me and where I was hiding, and they were probably watching me right then. I tried to look around my immediate area. But I could not see out of my left eye at all, and everything was blurry and out of focus through my right eye. I discovered that if I cocked my head and sort of tilted it up, I could partially see through the bottom of my right eye. I did not see anyone around me anywhere. I wondered if that meant that they were not there yet, or I just could not see them. I decided that I was not going to take my own life yet. I could do it…and I would do it,…but not yet. Not yet.

I looked all around me as best I could. I did not know if the NVA were on this side of the river yet, but I assumed they were. I was probably surrounded. Why hadn't they rushed me? I had to leave myself enough time so that when I saw them coming for me, I would be able to use my weapon on myself. I might try to take a couple of those bastards with me, but I could not take the chance of being surprised at the last minute and have my gun taken away from me. My .38 was the only guarantee I had against capture. My fear was not that they would shoot me and kill me. My fear was that they would *not* kill me.

I had to make a decision: should I stay here close to the crash site or try to move deeper into the jungle? If I moved further into the jungle, it would be harder for my people to find me. What about Kiser and Smoot? I did not want to move farther away from them, but I would not be able to stay here for very long. If I stayed here, I would be surrounded for sure. I probably already was. Foti and Osborn would give up looking for us soon, if they hadn't already. And who could blame them; there was no wrecked aircraft for them to see. The jungle was on fire; the river was on fire with JP-4; everything was on fire. They had made more low and slow "dry" passes looking for us than anyone had a right to expect. As soon as they determined there were no survivors, they would start blowing the hell out of this place with a vengeance.

I heard another aircraft overhead; this was one at altitude. I could not see it, and I could not tell if it was our C & C Huey or if we were beginning to get help. Maybe we were getting help already? But what could they do that Foti had not already done? I was not aware of any open areas around me for someone to slip in and pick me up. That only left hovering over the river, and that would be suicide. No one was going to attempt a rescue anywhere unless they saw me or made contact with me. I could not communicate by radio with any of our aircraft because my survival radio was now on the bottom of the river.

I now recognized the distinctive loud popping sound of the rotor blades of a Cobra in a high-speed dive. Foti was initiating a "gun" run. I knew this would eventually happen. Foti and Osborn had given us up for dead, and now they were going to make the NVA pay for what they had done here today. That was why I had not heard them for a while. They were not going to make any more low passes. They had climbed up to altitude and established a racetrack pattern, and now they were coming in on their first attack. Paul Foti would be flying from the back seat and firing rockets while Don Osborn, sitting in the front, would operate the chin turret firing the 7.62 mm minigun and the 40 mm grenade launcher.

A few minutes earlier I would not have believed that I could have been more afraid than I already was. Then the first rockets began to hit -- 17 pound warheads. "My God!" I realized for the first time how terrifying a rocket attack from a Cobra gunship really was! The rocket explosions were deafening, even though they were not actually impacting close to me. At least not yet. The trees and underbrush around me already popped and crackled from the fires that had been started by my crash. The exploding rockets were starting new fires. The constant sound of AK-47s, .30 cal. machineguns, and .51 cal. heavy machineguns had never diminished. Foti's first attack on the enemy did not seem to faze them. It was like throwing rocks at a hornet's nest. However, it did seem to me that the enemy firing was all coming from the north side of the river.

A gunship was in another gun run, but this could not be Foti again; it was too soon. This had to be a different Cobra; someone had joined 25. Someone else was in the fight. Yes! Then I realized that there were at least three Cobras up there, maybe more. I knew that Foti or the C & C bird, or probably both, had radioed back to Loc Ninh to "scramble" all of our aircraft.

A "scramble" meant that we had an aircraft down somewhere. Back at Song Be we had a siren just for that purpose. I had hated to hear that siren go off because it always meant that one of your buddies was in trouble. Our policy was to run to the closest aircraft, crank it up, and take off as soon as you had a crew. It did not matter whether it was your aircraft or your crew -- just get in the air and listen to the radios for a heading and location.

The rockets were getting closer, but of even more concern was the minigun fire. The minigun in the nose turret was used to cover the "break" after the gun run. The most vulnerable part of the gunship's attack was when he pulled out of the dive. It was then that he was most susceptible to ground fire since his rocket tubes only pointed forward. The minigun was used to spray down the area and "keep their heads down" as the aircraft broke off his attacking dive. The electrically powered spinning six barrels of the minigun spit out 7.62 mm at the rate of two thousand rounds per minute. It was indiscriminate. It did not know the "good" guys from the "bad" guys, and my people did not know that I was alive.

The Cobras were firing everything they had on their attacks: rockets, miniguns, grenade launchers. The fear of being captured here was now being overshadowed by the fear that my own people were going to kill me and not even know it. Suddenly I was startled by a metallic tinkling sound coming through the tree branches above me. It scared the hell out of me! I realized that it was the "spent" brass cartridges ejected from the minigun on the last pass. They had fallen through the tops of the trees and were bouncing off the branches on the way down. These were the empty shell casings, not the bullets, but that meant that my position was directly along the axis of their attack. There was no choice now; I had to move.

I started through the bushes and high grass and on into the jungle. The sun was beginning to get low. It was already dark under the thickest part of the jungle canopy. It would be dark everywhere soon.

The jungle here was more like a forest. There was room between the trees to walk, but the grass and the weeds were thick and difficult to move through. I thought that I was traveling generally west, and I needed to be going south. At that moment I was more interested in getting *away* from the immediate area than I was in getting *to* somewhere. I could not understand why the enemy had not found me yet. I walked with my revolver raised and cocked. I had never lowered the hammer from when I had first taken it out of the holster earlier. I was sure that I would run into the NVA any second. I hoped that I would see or hear them first. They would be hiding behind the next bush, or they would be around the next bend in the trail.

The vegetation the first one hundred meters from the river had been sparse trees and bushes, more forest than jungle. After the first hundred meters or so, the jungle began to get thick quickly. I did not know how far I had traveled or what was in front of me, but the sounds of machine gun fire and exploding rockets were getting farther away, and that made me feel safer. I did not know how I would find Kiser and Smoot, but I had made up my mind that I had to put distance between myself and the crash area. Of course, that also meant that I would be getting farther away from the rescue team that would eventually be put on the ground.

That presented another problem. How would I signal the rescue team? I did not have a radio. They would be ARVNs. I certainly did not want to startle them; they would be more nervous and jumpy than Americans. How would I get their attention without being shot by them, but at the same time not draw the attention of the wrong people? I could not speak Vietnamese. "God help me figure these things out." I did not have any infantry training. "Shit!" I wondered if I should have stayed near the crash site and tried to find Kiser and Smoot.

I suddenly came upon a river. I did not remember seeing another river in this area, but, then, other than today's flight, I had never seen this area. Was this the same river I had crashed in earlier or was this a different river? If this was the same river that I had crashed in, I might be traveling in circles! I had been following the sun as I traveled, and I was sure that I had been traveling generally west or maybe southwest. I did not believe that I was traveling in circles; the sun was in the same place and I was still moving away from the sounds of battle. If it was the same river, it must have turned ninety degrees or more and come around in front of me again. Is this the same river? Was I so shook up and confused that in the thickness of the jungle I had not been paying attention to the sun and had been traveling in a circle? I did not think so. Either way, I needed to cross the river.

I stayed in the trees above the bank and surveyed the river as best I could with my limited vision problem. I did not see anyone or any movement on either side of the river. "Damn." I hated to leave the trees and walk out into the open. As much as I did not want to do that, I still felt the urgency to get away from the area of the crash. I felt as though I were being chased or followed, but I did not hear anyone. I had to keep moving west or southwest, at least for now, and that meant crossing the river. I walked out of the bushes at the top of the bank and quickly waded into the water; I had no idea how deep it was.

I took off my shoulder holster and held it and my revolver above my head as I tried to keep my footing on the slippery rocks. The water was high on my chest almost to my neck. I did not want to have to swim. The current was not fast, but about halfway across the river I stepped in a hole and went under. I came up choking and swam until I could touch the bottom again. Somehow I managed not to lose my gun or holster, but both were soaked again, and I was no longer sure if my gun would even fire. Up until that moment I had not even considered that my revolver might not work. Actually, The Smith &Wesson Model 10 would probably work fine, but the ammunition might not.

I crawled out of the river and hurried up the bank and into the bushes. I was still traveling on adrenalin. I do not remember ever running, just walking quickly. I was already very tired. I was sore and burned and blind at least in the left eye and almost in the right. I felt beaten up as if I had been in a motorcycle or a car wreck.

I heard jets at altitude, but I could not tell what direction they were going or where they were holding. It was impossible now to see through the canopy of the trees.

I had worked with them enough to know that they would be in soon. Right now they would be getting their instructions from their FAC (forward air controller) who would have gotten all the pertinent information from Foti or the C & C bird. All that was left was to decide which direction would be best for their runs and what their barriers would be.

I heard the first jet come in screaming in his dive. There is no sound quite like a jet engine sucking in air, mixing it with fuel, and transforming that explosion of fire into pure power and thrust. The bombs began to hit almost immediately. The earth shook with the concussions. I did not know how far I had traveled from the crash or if I was far enough away to escape what was about to happen. I looked for something to hide behind, but there was nothing but trees. I wanted a hole. I realized that the bombs were actually hitting quite a distance away from me. I did not want them any closer.

I could not tell what type of "fast movers" were up there, but we usually worked with F-4 Phantoms. I also could not tell from the sound alone whether they were dropping napalm or "hard bombs," My guess was napalm, but I did not smell it.

I sat there in the shelter of the trees and listened to them put in three airstrikes, three separate attacks by two fighter-bombers. Any doubt that I may have had about leaving the area of the crash site was now gone. It was obvious to me that had I stayed near the aircraft and the river, I would now be dead. If Kiser and Smoot were still huddled by the river hiding, they were now dead. At least if we had been killed by the Cobra's rockets, our people would probably eventually find the bodies and our families would be notified.

If I had to die over here, I wanted my mother to know how I died. If I died right now, she would never know that I had survived the crash and that I was still trying to get away. That bothered me. For some reason it was important to me that she knew the exact circumstances of my death. However, now she would never know. She would be told that I died in the crash. She would never know how I died or where I died or when I died. Or that I had not given up.

I knew that did not make much sense. What real difference could it possibly make whether I died here where I was standing or back at the river? Whether I died now or as a result of the crash? But it made a difference to me. I wanted her to know that I had survived the crash and that I was still trying to get away when I was killed.

I looked down at the leaves surrounding me and thought, "All these leaves that no one cares about or even knows are here, will still be here after I'm dead. That doesn't seem right."

I started to walk again, and the sounds of the bombs and the burning jungle began to fade away. I do not know how far I walked. The terrain varied, but it was mainly thick forest, so I tried to stay on the trails. I came upon a large thicket of thorns. The thicket was probably twelve or fifteen feet wide by maybe twenty feet long.

I looked all around me as best I could with my one "good" eye. I was still blind in the left and most things were still blurry through the right. Tilting my head all the way back so I could look through the bottom of the eye helped; things seemed to be more in focus at a distance. Near vision was worse. I stood perfectly still. I did not see anyone around me, and I did not hear anything. The jungle was almost silent now, and darkness was closing in quickly.

I began to carefully and quietly push aside some of the thorns and make myself an entrance into the thicket. For the first time I noticed that my nomex flight gloves were missing. They would really be useful right now. I did not remember taking them off. They would not have come off in the crash, but when did I remove them and where were they now? I checked the leg pockets of my flight suit. No luck. I noticed my pant leg on my flight suit was torn. I looked in the hole but found no blood. That was good, but where the hell were my gloves? Don't tell me that in the excitement I took off my gloves and left them lying on the ground somewhere. "Shit! When did I do that?" I needed the bad guys to think that I was on the bottom of the river.

I worked quickly, separating and pushing more of the spiked stems apart, crawling deeper and deeper into my "cave" of briars. My work reminded me of a VC "sapper" working his way through concertina wire around a fire support base. I was continually stabbed and scratched by the thorns as I worked my way deep into the middle of the thicket;

all the while I expected someone to jump out of the bushes or come down the trail.

I knew the thicket of thorns did not offer me any real protection, but on the other hand, it would be dark soon and it would be impossible for someone to see me hiding inside the thicket. It would also be impossible for someone to get close to me without me hearing him. I would at least have some warning. I thought that no one would be willing to climb in those thorns as I had on the off chance of finding an American pilot hiding in there. I had tried to be careful not to leave any telltale clues that someone had disturbed the natural growth of the thorns.

All I wanted to do at that moment was sleep. I would worry about tomorrow tomorrow. I was terrified and hurt all over, but I was also exhausted. I curled up into the fetal position and prayed. Sleep came quickly.

Chapter Six

I grew up in the Midwest in east-central Indiana. Connersville was a small town that had quickly grown in industry after World War II. At the turn of the century the town's major claim to fame was being the home to several automobile factories that had long since gone out of business or at least left town. But in the years after World War II, many industries had grown up in and around the town. The largest employer was Philco Ford, with two factories in Connersville. Ford did not build cars in Connersville; they produced appliances, air conditioners, refrigerators, washers and dryers. They also produced air conditioners and condensers for Ford cars and trucks which they then shipped to Detroit.

My mother worked as a secretary there at one of the Ford plants in the maintenance office. This was after my parents divorced. She had been a stay-at-home mom, but after the divorce she found herself with two kids to take care of and no income. I was sixteen, and my little brother was five.

My father was a commercial pilot: single engine, fixed wing, and pure VFR (visual flight rules as opposed to IFR with sophisticated navigation and flight instruments). He flew pipeline patrol and he was very good at it. He patrolled a Gulf Oil pipeline that pumped crude oil from the Red River in Texas to Ohio. He flew that line down and back once a week. For awhile he also had a line from Philadelphia to Cleveland that he flew once a month.

He once turned in a "leak" that could not have been more than a ten or twelve inch dark spot right on the pipeline. The pipeline is buried roughly three feet deep and if there is a tiny hole or crack the pressure in the line will push the oil out eventually to the surface. Upon inspection by a ground crew, it was determined that the "leak" was actually where maintenance workers had cleaned out their paint brushes with turpentine after painting the pipeline markers at fence posts.

I spent many hours with him in 1142D, a green and white Cessna140 tail-dragger. He had taken the control wheel out of the right side so that he could put his maps and briefcase in the right seat without them interfering with the controls. When I went with him, he put me in the *left* seat and he sat in the right with no wheel. He watched the pipeline, and I flew. Sitting on two cushions to be able to see over the instrument panel, I was flying pipeline when I was twelve.

In high school I was a fair wrestler and a lousy student. It was not because of the teachers; the fault was all mine. I had no direction, no goals. I could not see any farther ahead than Friday night and the weekend. I worked at a fast food restaurant named Mac's, dated, wrestled, and spent way too much time with my friends. My very last priority was studying. My wrestling career ended abruptly my junior year after report cards came out. I was undefeated so far that season. I was crushed.

As graduation approached in 1968, several giant questions consumed me. Would I actually have enough credits to graduate? There was a real possibility I would not. And, if I did, what next? What then? Where was I going? Would I be drafted?

I had an aunt and uncle who had offered to pay my way through college if I would just go and try it. For a while I considered it. My grades and my GPA would never allow me to get into most colleges, but maybe I could get into a state college, maybe Ball State or Indiana State University. My mother and I visited Vincennes University, a two year college. I even applied and was accepted. But I did not really want to go.

Without a college deferment and no other reason to avoid the draft, I was prime meat for the Selective Service. I was beginning to consider flying in the Army. I needed a high school diploma and a good physical. I had already taken the draft physical in January when I had turned eighteen, and, of course, passed it just fine. One of my high school friends wanted me to join the Navy with him on the "buddy system." I wasn't much interested in the Navy; I would not be eligible for their flight program without a bachelor's degree. He joined without me, and, sure enough, got the submarine service that he wanted so badly.

I graduated from high school in May of 1968 still not knowing what I would do after graduation. I continued to think about flying in the Army. The local recruiter told me about something called the Warrant Officer Flight Program, and he was trying to get me to sign a contract for that.

I would go to Basic Training like everyone else, but then after graduation from basic, I would be sent to flight school, first at Ft. Wolters, Texas, and then Ft. Rucker, Alabama. That was it. That easy. I would be a warrant officer, whatever that was, and an Army Aviator. What a deal! I told him I would think about it, and I did. For a year I thought about it.

I did not go to college; I worked several jobs after graduation including Ford. But as a new hire at the bottom of the seniority list, I spent most of my "employment" time laid off. I continued to think about the Army. I was told that if I were drafted, I would not have any choice as to what branch of the service I joined or what my job would be. If I voluntarily joined, I would have the opportunity to choose what job I wanted in what branch (depending on test scores). Maybe I would not get drafted. Maybe if I got drafted, I would not go to Vietnam. Maybe pigs could fly.

Still, if I did get drafted, that was only for two years, and then I would be out. If I joined for flight school (and made it through) I would have a three-year obligation *after* my appointment as a warrant officer. Even with my limited math skills, I could figure out that two years was a lot less than over four. Basic training and flight school would take a little over a year.

I knew that if I did get drafted, I would do the honorable thing and serve. I would not go to Canada. My father was an Army medic in World War II. He served in Europe and then in the Pacific. He was on a troop ship getting ready for the invasion of Japan when the atomic bombs were dropped and Japan surrendered.

My step-grandfather had lied about his age when he was fifteen or sixteen, and joined the Army in 1917 after the United States entered World War I. He served in France, was seriously wounded, and came home a veteran without ever having shaved. I would not be going to Canada.

Anyway, kids from Indiana did not do that. No,…kids from Indiana found a *legal* way to avoid the draft. They went to college whether they wanted to or not. They said they were conscientious objectors. They purposely failed the military physical. They married their high school sweetheart (when that was still a deferment). They had a baby (when that was still a deferment). Others even claimed they were homosexuals. No, Indiana kids did not go to Canada.

I voluntarily enlisted in the Army in June of 1969 for the Warrant Officer Flight Program. I was confident that with my fixed wing flying experience, the Army would put me in airplanes, not helicopters. After all, I had flown pipeline patrol in a Cessna 140 when I was twelve.

Chapter Seven

I had enlisted in the Army for the Warrant Officer *Rotary* Wing Aviator Course. I wanted *Fixed* Wing (airplanes); the Army needed helicopter pilots. My contract guaranteed me that I would be sent to flight school upon graduation from basic training. Of course, there was no guarantee that I would make it *through* flight school. I was only guaranteed to be sent there. First I had to make it through basic training.

All enlistees earmarked for the Warrant Officer Flight Program were sent to Ft. Polk, Louisiana, for basic training. I was sworn in at Cincinnati, Ohio, and I was the only person on the bus from the recruitment center to the airport who was going to Ft. Polk. All of the other trainees were headed for either Ft. Dix, New Jersey; Ft. Leonard Wood, Missouri; or Ft. Knox, Kentucky.

Ft. Knox would have only been a four-hour drive from home. I did not have any idea where Ft. Polk was; I wasn't completely sure where Louisiana was.

I flew from Cincinnati to Love Field at Dallas, Texas, my first flight on a commercial airliner. At Dallas I had to change to a much smaller plane for the flight to Ft. Polk. The only carrier that flew into Polk was TTA, Trans Texas Airways, which I later found out was locally referred to as "Tinker Toy Airways." I wondered if the twin-engine commuter would even make it to Ft. Polk. It did, and I arrived late at night to the smell of pine trees and overwhelming humidity.

I quickly found that I hated basic training. I hated Ft. Polk, I hated Louisiana, and I hated the Army. I tried to tell myself that this was just the beginning and not what the Army would be like after graduation. And certainly not what it would be like as an officer. I tried not to lose sight of the ultimate goal, which was flight school. The *eight* weeks of basic training that the recruiter had always spoken of turned out to be ten. The time from arrival at the reception station to actually starting training was called a "zero" week and lasted usually seven to ten days, depending on when your basic training company was actually scheduled to begin.

Most of the basic training companies at Ft. Polk were at "South Fort," where the main post was located. That was where the swimming pool, the main PX, the theater, the golf course, the NCO and Officers' clubs, and all the other things that I would never see or be able to use were located.

However, I was assigned to C-5-2; Company "C," 5th Battalion, 2nd Basic Training Brigade. My brigade was located at "North Fort," which was the home of Army Infantry AIT (Advanced Individual Training), or "Tigerland" as it was known at Ft. Polk. All those poor bastards who had either been drafted, had done poorly on the aptitude tests, or in some cases, actually had enlisted for the infantry, went to Tigerland.

Even though we were a *basic* training company that happened to be at North Fort, our company commander, who had been in Special Forces in Vietnam, apparently felt the need to train us as if we were all going to go to the infantry. Many of the people in my company were, but there were also a large number of guys who, upon graduation from basic, would be going on to Texas as Warrant Officer Candidates. Whether it was true or not, we all felt that we would have had it a lot easier in a basic training company at South Fort.

The drill sergeants were, for the most part, soldiers who had recently returned from Vietnam. Many of the younger ones had been drafted. They were just putting in their time until their enlistment was up. They hated the Army, and they hated us -- or at least they seemed to.

The older sergeants were mostly career Army -- "lifers." They had already put in one or two tours in Vietnam and would be going back.

They hated us because most of us would not be making the Army a career. It was, after all, their Army, and we were just visiting.

Some of the drill sergeants were hard on us because they truly wanted us to learn what would become life-saving skills; others were just sadistic bastards. They particularly hated the National Guard and the Army Reserve trainees because they knew that after basic and AIT, those guys would be going home to a life of drilling one weekend a month and two weeks in the summer.

They also knew that several of us in the company were marked for Warrant Officer Flight School and would someday (maybe) be officers. They all seemed to have a story about some damn warrant officer gunship pilot who had fucked up and fired on "friendlies" and killed a friend of theirs. They apparently intended to punish every future army aviator for that.

The most professional and the very best of them was Senior Drill Sergeant John Dutra. He could not have weighed more than a 120 pounds soaking wet, and he was the toughest of them all. But there was compassion underneath that hardened exterior. He really truly wanted to help us prepare for a surreal world he knew we would someday be immersed in. He wanted us to survive in that world. I listened especially carefully to everything SDS Dutra said because I knew that if he said it, it was true, and it would probably help me someday.

The two-and-half months at Ft. Polk dragged by. I was miserable. I wondered every day if I had made a terrible mistake joining the Army. I almost forgot during the ten weeks why I was there. It was hard to remember the "big picture" goal: flight school and being an Army helicopter pilot. And that this hell that I was going through right now was only temporary, just one step in the process. The days were so long and the nights were so short; I was hungry and exhausted most of the time.

One day we trainees came back to the barracks after a very long and grueling day of training to find that while we were gone, the drill sergeants had wrecked both floors of our two-story WWII barracks. We had left the building in perfect condition as we did every day: floors highly polished and buffed; all beds had carefully folded "hospital corners" on our blankets and sheets; all the contents of the foot lockers precisely measured and displayed; wall locker uniforms flawlessly hung, -- everything.

The drill sergeants had turned over our bunk beds and tossed our mattresses everywhere, dumped our foot lockers all over the floor, thrown everything in our wall lockers on the floor, and dumped the "butt cans" (#10 food cans for the purpose of safely getting rid of smoked cigarettes). The butt cans were painted red and placed on every other vertical post that held up the ceiling. There were two inches of water in the can to safely extinguish thrown-away butts. Everyone smoked.

The beautifully polished and buffed floor was now scratched from the overturned bunk beds and tossed foot lockers. Everything was covered with shaving lotion they had taken from our lockers. It would take us all night to get everything cleaned and ready for inspection. That meant no sleep. There would undoubtedly be another unannounced inspection first thing in the morning. I was not sure how this could possibly help prepare us for combat in the future, although I certainly did want to kill the drill sergeants.

There were other guys in my company who were also going to the Warrant Officer Flight Program: Paul Hendren, John "Butch" Cleary, Carl Nacca, and Hugh Pettit, to name a few. We quickly found each other and sought support from each other. My closest friend, however, was a National Guard trainee named Kenny Funderburk. Not only was Ken from Louisiana, but he was actually from the local Leesville area.

He took me home with him on a weekend pass, and his mother and his family were wonderful to me. Ken even set me up with a date.

C-5-2 graduated in late August 1969. Warrant Officer Candidates were sent home on a two week leave, with orders to report back to Ft. Polk where we would be transported by charter buses to Ft. Wolters, Texas. We trainees had almost no contact with other basic training companies at North Fort and no contact at all with companies at South Fort. It had not occurred to me that there were other basic training companies graduating at the very same time as we were each with their complement of Warrant Officer Candidates. There were a lot of buses.

Chapter Eight

The two weeks at home in between graduation from basic training and returning to Ft. Polk passed in an instant. I hated to have to go back to Ft. Polk; I never wanted to see that place again. I had a terrible feeling that once back there, the drill sergeants would find some way to screw us over and keep us there. I was anxious to get to Texas and get on with it. I was anxious to fly.

We spent one night at Polk and then were loaded on charter buses for the trip to Ft. Wolters, Texas, located roughly 50 miles west of Fort Worth. The hours on the bus drifted by with the scenery. The forests and swamps of west Louisiana and east Texas quickly became gently rolling grasslands and prairies. We passed through Dallas and Fort Worth and on to Weatherford and Mineral Wells. The country was beautiful.

The TAC (Tactical Advisers and Counselors) officers were waiting for us as we got off the buses, and they immediately tore into us. I mistakenly thought we had left the screaming, and yelling, and bullying behind with graduation from basic training. They were just like the drill sergeants we had left behind at Ft. Polk, except these were warrant officers. That was the first time I had actually ever seen one.

We were placed in a holding company called "snowbirds" and moved into old World War II barracks until our Warrant Officer Candidate company was ready to receive us. In the meantime it became obvious that the goal of the TAC officers was to weed out as many candidates as possible, as quickly as possible, before the Army invested much money in our training. If they spotted a flaw in our behavior or our attitude or the way we looked, we were a target for all to pounce on. We were then earmarked for elimination. I decided that was the real meaning of TAC officer, it was short for "Attack Officer."

We spent our time in snowbirds trying to learn everything we possibly could to be ready for when we were sent to our Warrant Officer Candidate company. No flight training yet, no flight manuals, nothing regarding helicopters or flying. Most of us had never seen a warrant officer candidate before and we tried to quickly learn the placing of different unfamiliar items on the unique uniform and how they were to be worn.

We had learned most of the tricks of how to build a good spit-shine on a pair of boots and the best way to remove the lacquer from brass so it could be polished correctly while we were in basic training. But the WOC program took all that to a much higher level. We learned how to take our brass belt buckles apart so we could polish the *inside* of the buckle. We measured and folded and rolled our socks perfectly. Razors and toothbrushes had to look as if they had never been used, but the penalty for keeping a "display" razor and hiding the real razor you were using was severe.

Your two pair of boots had to be "notched" on the heels to prevent you from wearing the same pair every day and leaving a perfectly shined "display" pair in your locker, (the pair with one notch was to be worn on odd calendar days, two notches on even calendar days.). We learned to clean and place all of our personal toiletries exactly in the right position in our lockers where we knew they would be measured. Everything had to be perfect.

The concept we were being taught was "attention to detail," something we were told would be very important if and when we ever became Army helicopter pilots. There is a reason why the airlines like to hire military-trained pilots.

My group spent roughly two weeks in snowbirds before we went "up on the hill" to our company. By then we had lost two entire barracks full of candidates who had voluntarily quit the program or been kicked out. The ones who quit were sick of the harassment, sick of being screamed at, sick of the expectation of perfection. Of course, if you quit, you were not out of the Army, you were just out of the program.

During the two weeks we were in snowbirds, there was a string of fatal accidents. We were not flying yet, but word quickly spread. Two of the accidents involved mid-air collisions; one of the aircraft fell to earth near the Holiday Inn in Mineral Wells. Several candidates and instructors died. I wondered if that accident rate and death toll were considered normal. I called my mother to tell her that I was safe on the off chance that word of the accidents might get into the national news and reach far away Indiana.

In 1969 there were ten Warrant Officer Candidate companies at Ft. Wolters, each with five flights (platoons). Each of the companies had a particular color associated with it. I was assigned to the 9th WOC; we were the "Tan Hats," class 70-15. We each wore a tan ball cap with our two-piece nomex flight suits or our heavily starched fatigues. Some day embroidered "solo" wings would be sewn on the front of those caps. Most candidates soloed somewhere around the thirteen-to-fifteen hour level. If we were wearing dress greens, we wore a tan disc under the WOC brass on our barracks cap.

The actual Warrant Officer Candidate company barracks were very nice three-story concrete block buildings. Not like those two-story wooden fire traps in snowbirds and basic training. We saw to it that the buildings were immaculately cleaned; the concrete slab floors were waxed and polished to the point they were almost dangerous to walk on.

Ft. Wolters had civilian contracted KPs (kitchen police; cooks and dishwashers). The food was excellent, but more important, that meant that there were no *candidate* KPs. It was not like basic training; the Army wanted to make sure that candidates received enough sleep to safely keep up with their flying duties and studies. Mistakes made by trainees in basic training due to sleep deprivation were serious enough, but mistakes made by sleep-deprived candidates learning to fly were worse. The accident rate was high enough.

The nine months of flight training in the Army Warrant Officer Rotary Wing Aviator Course (WORWAC) was actually divided into two phases: five months of Primary Flight Training at Ft. Wolters, Texas, followed by four months of Advanced Flight Training (if you made through Ft. Wolters) at either Ft. Rucker, Alabama, or for some, Ft. Hunter-Stewart, Georgia. Most went to "Mother Rucker."

The first of the five months spent at Ft. Wolters was devoted to "ground school," never touching a real helicopter. We heard them and saw them fly over but we were not allowed anywhere near them. Every day was spent in a classroom. Finally we met our IP (Instructor Pilot) and began to fly. Four out of five flights (platoons) in a company flew the Hughes TH-55, what many referred to as the "Mattel Messerschmitt." It was tiny, but we really hoped it was better built and more substantial than a toy. The fifth flight was made up of all "tall" guys who would not fit into a TH-55; so they flew either the Bell OH-13 or the Hiller OH-23.

The first instructor took us from "this is a helicopter" to soloing and then passed us on to another IP for more involved flying. Hovering was the toughest part, and most of us could "fly" reasonably well long before we mastered hovering. We flew half the day, either mornings or afternoons, and had classroom instruction the other half.

Our "officer" class counterparts (lieutenants, captains, and a few majors) were going through the same flight school curriculum that we were but did not attend any "how to be an officer" classes. They had already gone through OCS, or ROTC, or even West Point. They were being treated and paid as officers, whereas candidates received E5 pay (largely because of the extra cost of uniforms, laundry, and sewing) but had no rank. WOCs were treated as if we were the lowest "low lifes" on earth. The officers put in their days of flying or ground school and then went home to the BOQ (Bachelor Officers Quarters) or their wives. Candidates went home to clean the barracks.

As I said, the country was beautiful. This was north-central Texas. We learned to do "pinnacle" approaches to high mesas and land there in tight "confined" areas. We did some "cross country" flying and some formation flying. By the time we graduated, I really liked the TH-55.

Ft. Rucker was located deep in the "Old South" in the southeastern corner of Alabama, a half hour drive from the Florida border. The last few weeks at Ft.Wolters, we had been "senior" candidates, indicated by a black stripe on a prominent orange plastic pocket tab. We were given the respect that that achievement deserved, at least by the WOCs, but at Rucker we were considered "intermediate" candidates, and we started all over again at the bottom.

The harassment continued, but there was a very subtle difference. We had now completed five months of a nine-month program. The Army had spent a lot of money on us. Unlike Ft. Wolters, where candidates were tossed out for almost anything, at this point in the program the Army wanted us to succeed. We were gradually given more freedom, and the level of harassment decreased, especially after we made it through "instruments," the first major hurdle at Ft. Rucker.

The training schedule at Ft. Rucker began with four weeks of instrument training, learning to fly without being able to see outside the aircraft. We were not expected to qualify for a "standard" instrument ticket but instead learn enough to receive a "tactical" ticket. That level of training would hopefully teach us enough about flying on instruments to keep the aircraft right side up in the clouds or in bad weather.

I had a terrible time with instruments and eventually was "set back" in training two weeks. As a result, I was transferred from my Class 70-17 (what had graduated Class 70-15 at Ft. Wolters) to Class 70-19, the company that was two weeks behind us. My group of friends, some with whom I had come all the way from basic training with, was now scheduled to graduate two weeks before me.

My original class had just attained "senior" status, which I lost temporarily by being set back. I kept my mouth shut and swallowed my pride, thankful to still be in the program. For the most part, the guys in the new company accepted me. Michael Lukow became my new roommate and closest friend.

I made it through instruments, and we went on to transition into the mainstay of the United States Army helicopter fleet, the turbine-powered UH-1, better known as the Huey. We flew A, B, and D model Hueys, in no particular order, never knowing which model aircraft we would be assigned the following day. The newest (and latest and greatest) model was the UH-1H, but all the "H" models went from the factory in Fort Worth straight to Vietnam. We would soon be meeting them there.

The training became more intense as we neared graduation, but for the most part, we now normally had evenings free (unless we were flying) and weekends off. We were seniors again, but unlike our senior status at Ft. Wolters, *this* time we were at the end of the program.

We spent as many weekends as we could at Panama City Beach, Florida. I could leave my barracks and be on the beach with a bottle of wine in an hour and a half. I never got tired of sitting in the sand staring at the Gulf of Mexico.

My friends and I stayed at a place called the El Centro Motel run by a sweet old gal named Ginny Albritton. She called us "her pilots," and she was very kind to us. The El Centro was located across the highway from the beach where Hwy 79 intersected the main road. There was a convenience store in the "V" of the intersection, and the El Centro was across the road on the inland side.

Ginny rented me a very small room for $7.00 a night. I am sure that it used to be a maintenance room, more like a closet; there was no room number on the door and it was certainly too small for guests, but it had a small bed and a window air conditioner (in the wall, there was no window). It was fine for me and in my price range.

Most of the tourist girls did want much to do with us. Our short haircuts and pure white skin did not leave much doubt that we were military. We contrasted greatly with the well-tanned long-haired college-boy crowd. They associated us with the war that they had now come to hate and that their male friends had somehow managed to stay out of. To them *we* were the enemy.

Our best bet for trying to date was to meet local girls: waitresses, hotel maids, store workers. They would also be here the following week, the vacationing tourists would not. Not that I had much luck with that either. Well,...there was one girl.

Warrant Officer Rotary Wing Aviator Course 70-19 graduated in the middle of July 1970. I had been in the Army a little over a year, roughly thirteen months. We had to be officers to be Army aviators, so we received our appointment as Army Reserve Warrant Officers on the 13th of July and "officially" graduated and received our wings on the following day, the 14th. We also received our orders for out next duty station. Out of the entire class, one man got orders for South Korea, one for Alaska, two for Germany, and all the others received orders for RVN, the Republic of Vietnam.

The large number of new warrant officer aviators being sent to Vietnam was no surprise to us; we assumed *everyone* would get orders to go there. That was the only surprise, that there was anyone who did *not* get orders for Vietnam. It had been understood from the beginning that upon graduation from flight school we would receive our "bars "as a WO1, our wings, and our orders for Vietnam.

I went home to Indiana for a thirty-day leave to see my family and friends and to say goodbye.

Part II

11 March 1971

Day Two

Chapter Nine

I awoke around eight or nine o'clock judging by the sun. I had hoped that I would awake to find out that all of this experience had just been a terrible nightmare. It took me a while to realize where I was and how I had gotten here; then the stark terror set in again. The gripping, barely controllable fear was back. I had successfully fought off the panic the day before, but it was always there close by.

I was really sore now, much worse than yesterday. I ached all over. The flies, gnats, and mosquitoes were all over me. They were attracted to the fluids seeping out of my burns. The skin had not had a chance to scab over yet, and I could not wipe the flies off without getting my dirty hands in my wounds.

I could not see my face, but I could feel the flies and other insects walking on it, and I could see them buzzing past my right eye. I tried to swat them away, but it was a futile effort. In a fit of desperation I slapped my burned left wrist with my right hand and permanently imbedded the mosquitoes that had been feeding there into my unhealed burn.

All of this swatting and slapping accomplished nothing. There were dozens of mosquitoes and even more flies. They would win, and I would wear myself out. I also had to stay quiet and concentrate on listening to the jungle. I resigned myself to the fact that I had to ignore them. Regardless of how maddening they were and how uncomfortable they made me feel I was powerless to stop them. I would have to let them feed on me.

I also knew I would be infected with whatever Asian diseases those mosquitoes were carrying. Tropical diseases were the least of my worries, at least for now.

I checked my eyes again; I was still blind in the left eye. I was getting some light through it as I had the day before, but it was somehow different. I still could not see anything out of it. Everything up close was still very blurry through my right eye. I would have to wait until I crawled out of the thorns to check my distance vision.

I sat and listened to the jungle. It was very quiet. Either the animals were afraid of something that was out there or they had all left the area. I decided I was in no hurry to leave the relative security of the thicket of thorns; I would sit and listen awhile.

I sat there in silence. I had slept on my shoulder holster, and my pen-flare gun had dug into my side during the night. As I looked at the flare gun that I had attached to my holster, it suddenly occurred to me to inventory the rest of my equipment and see what I had with me. Why had I not thought of this yesterday? Shit.

I took off my shoulder holster and began to look at the things I had attached to it months ago. I had a folding Buck knife in a leather sheath that my father had given me to take to Vietnam. I had run one of the straps of my holster through the belt loop of the sheath, and it was still there. The knife was secure in its place with a leather flap that snapped closed over it.

I had buckled the nylon wristband of a small survival compass to the knife sheath's belt loop. It did not appear to be broken. I could not believe that I had not even thought about the compass yesterday! I guessed that there had been so much confusion that somehow I had not even remembered it. My only thought yesterday had been to escape, but how could I have been so stupid? I did all that traveling the day before by watching the sun, and the whole time I had a compass. What an idiot. I must have been in shock. I unfastened the compass from the sheath, and knowing I would be carrying my revolver raised in my right hand, fastened the compass's wristband around my left wrist below the burn.

I had wedged a flare gun in between two of the straps of my holster and with it six "pen" flares. Finally, I had about 20 rounds of .38 cal.

ammunition that I had wrapped a small plastic bag and fastened to my holster. This was in addition to the six bullets in the gun; I was amazed that everything I had put together was still there.

I looked at the things I had laid out as I inspected them. I had a handgun and 26 bullets, a pen-flare gun and six flares, a knife, and a compass. I wished I had my M-16.

Most of my survival gear was with the aircraft on the bottom of the river. There was not enough room up front for everything we carried with us, so we had to put most of our survival equipment in the back with Smoot. In theory, upon being shot down, we would autorotate into an open area somewhere, and we would have the time to get all of our equipment out of the bird. That would have been the ideal situation.

I had my own M-16 with a 20-round magazine. I also carried an NVA ammo pouch with ten 20-round magazines in it. I did not know what that communist-made ammo pouch was really for, but its flapped pockets with their wooden buttons was perfect for ten 20-round M-16 magazines. That was over 200 rounds of ammunition just for me.

I had had a PRC 90 UHF survival radio, a survival mirror, and a lensatic compass, but all of that was now on the bottom of the river and worthless to me. The only thing I was able to get out of the aircraft was the shoulder holster I was wearing.

I put the shoulder holster back on. I would have traded everything on the holster for a canteen cup of water. That was what I really needed; my throat was scorched and dry. I had to find water.

I had been awake for what I thought was roughly an hour. I thought it was probably around nine or ten o'clock. It was time to get started. I had slept well, all things considered. I hated to leave the relative security of my "den" of thorns, but it was time to get moving, and I had to find water.

I quietly crawled out of the thicket and into the open. The jungle was absolutely silent. It was mostly triple canopy, but enough light was passing through the branches of the trees above me to be able to clearly see -- that is, if I had been able to clearly see.

I looked at my newly found compass. It was about the size of a quarter and looked like something that had come out of a box of Cracker Jack. I wondered if it really worked. I held the face as still as I could while I turned around slowly in a circle. The needle continued to point in the same direction regardless of which way I faced or turned. It also seemed to agree with where I thought north was judging by the sun. Maybe it did work.

I needed to travel southeast if I was going to intersect Highway 13. I did not have a map, but I tried to visualize where I was in reference to the road and the river. I knew that Highway 13 crossed the river at the bombed-out bridge and then turned to the west. I had been somewhere to the northwest of there when I was shot down. But how far north and how far west? Foti had me on a southerly heading when I was hit, but I was too low to be able to see where I was in relation to any landmarks around me. I was sure that I was north of the river, but was I south of that east-west section of the road?

I wondered how far I had traveled the day before. I did not see how I could have moved more than four or five hundred meters from the crash site. That movement was almost all generally west.

What about the river that I had crashed in? Did that river feed into the river with the bridge? Was that the same river? That was what I needed: I needed to find the river with the blown-up bridge. I decided the goal would be to find the river which had to be south of me. Once I found the river, I would follow it east to the bridge. When I found the bridge, I would know where I was. I would cross the river and follow Highway 13 to Snuol. If I was actually north of Highway 13, then by traveling south I would hit the road first and that would be fine, too --

that is, if I could get that far without being caught. OK, it was a plan. I had to find the river.

I needed water desperately, and I had no idea how long it would be until I found the river. It was already hot, and I knew I would get dehydrated quickly, not to mention my burned throat. It was the dry season, and water was going to be difficult to find. The river I was looking for could be the only water in the area.

I turned around again until I was facing southeast. I looked to see if there was something distinguishing, something at a distance to use as a landmark to walk to. Ideally I needed a tall tree or some other land feature a half mile or so away to get a good bearing on. Once I was sure that I had a good bearing, I would walk to the tree and not look at my compass again until I got there. Then I would take another bearing on another tree and just keep repeating the process.

I had two problems right away. First was my vision. The compass dial was very small, and I could see only reasonably well at a distance, my near vision was still blurry. The other problem was the jungle itself. As long as the jungle was as thick as it was here, I would never be able to get a bearing on a landmark at a distance. I could only see about twenty yards at the very most in any direction. I would have to do the best I could.

I looked at what was supposed to be southeast according to the compass. I saw the top of a tree I thought I would be able to continue to see as I walked to it; it seemed to be a little taller than those near it. That tree was on a heading of south-southeast. That would work. I thought that if I kept moving I should find the river within a few hours and the road by the end of the day. That was, of course, if I did not get captured first. That was a big "if." I pulled my .38 out of its holster, cocked it, and started to walk to the tree. There was a trail that generally ran the direction I needed to go. The consensus of army doctrine and survival manuals was never to walk on a trail when you knew the enemy controlled the area. For that matter, those same manuals made it clear that you should hide in the daytime and travel only at night. I wondered if the guys who wrote the manuals had ever been in my situation.

It would have been impossible to travel at night in this jungle. The triple canopy shut out a large amount of light at midday. By late afternoon it got dark, and at night I quite literally could not see my hand in front of my face. If I did not use the trails and instead attempted to move though the "bush," it would take me ten times as long to get anywhere, and I would no longer be able to see my landmark tree. I decided to stay on the trail.

I took the most southern branch every time I came to a fork in the trail. The trails kept turning back to the west, and I did not want to go west. I did not even want to go southwest. The trail I was on did the same thing: it was gradually turning more and more west and less and less south. I decided to stay with it a little while longer to see if I would come upon a trail that was more suitable to what I needed.

I walked for probably 15 or 20 minutes, and the trail was now taking me west. I had to make a decision. If I left the trail and started out "cross-country," it would be rough and slow, and I did not have machete. Even if I had one, I would not want to make a lot of noise hacking my way along.

On the other hand, I could not stay on a trail that was taking me the wrong direction just because it was easier. I walked another five minutes while I thought it over, and sure enough, the trail ever so slightly turned more to the northwest. Shit. I decided I had no choice. I looked at the side of the trail; it was thick. I backtracked and retraced my steps back to a point where the trail was still running mainly west. I spotted a tree in the distance that seemed to be a little taller than those around it. That would be my landmark.

The tree I had chosen was very close to a south-southeast heading, but once I started into the jungle, I had no way of knowing how long it would be before I would be able to see the tree again, or for that matter, if I would *ever* be able to see the tree again or even recognize it once I got to it. I might lose my bearings and never find the tree. That would be a risk I would have to take.

I took one last look at my "target" tree and stepped off the trail into the snarled vines and brush. I pushed vines out of my way or stepped through them or stepped over them. I tried to move quietly, but I probably sounded like a fucking elephant going through there. I had no idea how far I had come or how long I had been at it, but I quickly became exhausted. The sun was high. I still had no water. I had not had a drink since I stepped in the hole crossing the river. I sat down to take a break and rethink what I was doing.

I checked my compass course again; there was a solid wall of brush, bushes, and vines in front of me. I turned around and looked in the direction I had come from. I could not see a hole, or trampled down brush, or any other clue as to where I had come from or how I had gotten in here. It was as if the jungle had closed in around me and swallowed me up once and for all. The feeling of near panic was coming back; I should have stayed with the trail.

There was no point in going back. It would be just as difficult to fight my way back through the brush to try to find the trail again as it would be to fight my way forward. Still, there was something reassuring about knowing that the trail was back there somewhere. But so were the "bad guys."

I had no way of knowing what was in front of me. Maybe they had heard me and knew I was in here and they were just waiting for me to find my way out. What if there were miles and miles of this same stuff? What if there were no more trails out there in front of me? There had to be, didn't there? This mission had taken us the farthest north that I had ever been, but I was somewhat familiar with the terrain to the south, and I knew there were trails and side roads and some open areas. I just did not know how far south of me that was. This could not last forever; there had to be an end to this. I had to keep trying.

I stood up and looked at the obstacle. It seemed impregnable. Shit. I got down on my hands and knees and began to crawl. I am not going to stay here, I told myself. I did not survive the crash and escape yesterday just to be lost out here forever in this fucking maze. I prayed to God to help me find my way out.

I worked my way through the tangled mess of vines and weeds and bushes for hours. I stood up and walked when I was able, but most of the time I crawled. The thorns punctured and tore at my skin. Branches I pushed out of my way flipped back and smacked me in the face and eyes. I bumped into and got caught on things that I did not even see with my limited vision. I became frustrated and discouraged. I did not seem to be getting any closer to anything that I needed. I hurt all over, and I was thirsty.

When was the last time I'd had water? I almost drowned in the crash. Then I got another mouthful when I stepped in the hole in the river. When was that? That was yesterday sometime in the late afternoon. No wonder I was thirsty. I had to find water.

I stopped and looked at my revolver. I had been crawling with the hammer down, so it would not snag as much in the underbrush. I sat and looked at the weapon. "I could end all of this right now," I thought to myself. No more struggling, no more fear. I was just postponing the inevitable anyway. There was, after all, no way out of this predicament. Even if I found my way out of this maze, the outcome would be the same. There was no way to stay out here without being caught. I had no food, no water, no radio, no map. The entire area was crawling with the enemy, and we had no "friendlies" on the ground. It was an impossible situation.

I decided I would not use my gun on myself, at least not now. No matter how depressed I had become, I had to push that thought out of my mind. It may very well come to that, but not yet. Yesterday, in the moments immediately after the crash, I was sure I only had minutes, possibly seconds to live. Death or capture was imminent and inevitable. But I was wrong. I was not killed or captured. Somehow God kept that from happening. That was 24 hours ago; look how far I'd come. I should have been killed or captured yesterday. Hell, I should have been killed in the crash! I couldn't give up now. I was not going to give those bastards the satisfaction of winning by default. I prayed to God to get me out of there.

I had to find water. I had to find my way out of the labyrinth of knotted vines and vegetation and find water. I checked my compass again even though I was not able to see more than a few yards. South-southeast -- that was my way out. I had wasted enough time. I got on my hands and knees and started to crawl again.

Chapter Ten

I never did find the tree that I had taken the original bearing on. As the hours went by, the jungle or forest or whatever it was began to change. The underbrush was still thick, and I was still crawling much of the time, but the canopy above me was thinning out, and as it did, more and more light was filtering through to the ground. After a while the canopy above me was completely gone. I was now in daylight, but I was still fighting my way through a wall of thick vegetation. Suddenly I broke out of my jungle within a jungle and found myself not only out of the maze but also out of the forest. I was now on the edge of a clearing. My morale immediately improved. I sat down to rest and surveyed the clearing from behind some bushes just inside the tree line.

I realized for the first time that I was hungry. When was the last time I had eaten? Yesterday was March the 10th; but I did not eat yesterday. I had gotten a cup of coffee that morning on the way to the flight line, but I had decided to pass on the eggs. The last time I ate was the day before that. But I could not remember if I had eaten that evening or earlier in the day.

I wondered what day of the week it was. I had grown up in a culture of a five-day workweek and a two-day weekend. Even the stateside army was set up that way. However, here in the war, there were no weekdays or weekends, and no holidays. I was either scheduled to fly, or I was not; Saturday and Sunday had nothing to do with it. Every day was the same.

I had flown all day on Christmas. A sister unit (Echo Troop) had lost a Cobra north of Lai Khe in the middle of the night on Christmas Eve, and a bunch of us from Apache Troop were sent over there to help in the search. We looked for it for two days. The aircraft was finally found a week later. It had flown into the ground on a gun run. The aircraft might have been shot down, but "target fixation" was the suspected killer, a common problem for gunship pilots working at night.

Cobra pilots were temporarily blinded when they fired their rockets due to the tremendous bright light of the rocket motors. Unless there was a moon, it was almost impossible to see the top of the jungle at night; therefore, the Cobra AC would find it very difficult to judge when to start pulling out of his dive in a gun run. If a pilot became too caught up in the excitement of the moment and the mission, he could easily not pull out of the dive in time. Sometimes they did not pull out at all. I was glad that as a Scout pilot I rarely had to fly at night.

I flew all day on New Year's. I flew most of my birthday in January. And we all flew, and fought, through the Christmas "Truce."

There was no reason to know what *day* of the week it was; however, we still needed to know the date. I had to fill out and date the numerous pages of the aircraft logbook every day. I needed to know if it was close to payday; we were paid once a month. I tried to keep up on family birthdays at home. And, of course, I had to know how close I was to the long awaited and far away DEROS (Date Estimated to Return from Overseas) date.

I had been born on a Friday. In fact, I had been born on Friday the 13th. I wondered if I would die on a Friday.

Maybe I *did* have something to eat. I felt in my left chest pocket for my cigarettes. I reached in my pocket and removed what was left of a half-used package of Marlboros. It was now a soggy mess. I had been smoking three packs a day for several months, and I always had an extra pack in the left leg pocket of my flight suit. That package had not been opened, and maybe the river had not ruined it. It was not in as bad a shape as the first pack, but it was also ruined. The unbroken cellophane wrapper had not protected it, and those cigarettes were also mush.

I pinched a small amount of the tobacco from the first pack between my fingers and tasted it. I realized that I was not *that* hungry and spit it out. There was not much left of the first pack, so I shredded it and sprinkled it over the ground. I kept the unopened pack and put it back in my pocket in case I changed my mind later.

I really wanted to smoke a cigarette, but even if I had a dry one, I would not have been willing to take the chance of firing one up, at least not yet. The smell of cigarette smoke is very distinctive and can carry for a long distance.

I sat there at the edge of the clearing for 15 or 20 minutes; it was time to move again. I had listened carefully to the jungle around me and watched the edge of the clearing for any sign of movement. I was satisfied that I was alone. I took a sighting on the compass and picked a place in the bushes on the other side of the clearing. That would be where I would enter. I wondered if this was a big mistake; those few seconds of exposure could get me killed…or worse, captured.

So far, the thickness of the jungle and its hindrance to visibility had kept me from being detected. Maybe I should wait until dark. Maybe I should not go out into the clearing at all and instead circle around the clearing staying in the trees. But I knew I had to find water. I walked out of the thicket that I had struggled with for so much of the day and into the clearing. I stayed low and hurried, but I did not run. It was late afternoon. I thought I must have been on the ground now for at least 24 hours. I quickly covered the 20 yards of clearing and ducked into the bush again.

The area here was thick but nothing like what I had been crawling through for hours. This was more like thick forest than jungle. I took a bearing on my compass and took note of a tree about 50 yards away. I tried to keep it in sight as I started walking towards it.

I had noticed that there were no sounds in the jungle -- nothing, not even birds. Was that normal? I grew up on *Tarzan* movies with Johnny Weismuller. I thought there was supposed to be a lot of noise in the jungle. I assumed I was making too much noise, and the animals heard me coming. However, even when I sat still for long periods of time while I rested, there were no sounds at all. In fact, it was very peaceful. If I had been in a squirrel woods back in Indiana, I would have actually enjoyed it. I still expected that peace to end any moment in a hail of gunfire. My gun was still in my hand and cocked. The North Vietnamese had to be here somewhere; they controlled the entire area.

I had found a trail that ran generally south to southeast, so I followed it. At least it was going the right direction. The trail turned from time to time, but it stayed pretty much on my course. As I walked, I finally noticed that the ravine to my right, running parallel to the trail, was actually a streambed. I guessed I had not noticed it because it did not have any water in it. When I finally realized what it was, I quickly walked over to it, slipped down the bank, and stepped down into it. It was a stream for sure, but it was absolutely dry. Maybe there was some water left in it somewhere.

I was getting excited as I hurriedly walked down the stream. I hoped that somewhere I would find some little pool of water that had not dried up yet. That turned out not to be the case. There was nothing. I could not even find a damp spot. I continued to walk down the streambed. I had checked the compass again, and it was going mainly south to southeast. There did not seem to be much difference in walking in the stream or on the trail. Both were easy walks, they were both going the correct direction for the moment, and I certainly had a better chance of finding water in this little branch than I did on the trail. However, I was at a tactical disadvantage walking in the streambed, the trail being on higher ground 10 or 12 feet above me.

I suddenly heard an aircraft in the distance. The distinctive whop whop whop of a single Huey at altitude. There was too much canopy above me here to see where he was or tell which direction he was going. I was not imagining it; he was up there. I had no radio or survival mirror. I regretted that I had not fastened the mirror on my holster along with everything else. Of course it would not do me any good with this canopy.

I considered the flare gun, but I weighed the chances of him being in a position to see that small pen-flare against the loud crack it would make when I fired it. I decided not to chance it. It would have been different if I could actually see the aircraft and know that he was facing my direction when I fired it. I hoped I would have another opportunity. In the meantime, my morale was spiraling down again.

I began to realize there had not been any water flowing in that stream for a long time. The longer I followed it, the more disappointed I became. I had read or heard somewhere that water will pool in the channel of a dried-up stream, sometimes just below the surface. I paid close attention to the outside turns of the creek where the channel should have been. The outside turns may have been a little deeper, but not by much; there were no deep turns.

I decided it was worth a try, so I began to dig in the lowest place I could find in what I thought had been the channel. I dug with my hands and with the help of a stick. Once again, I realized how much easier this would have been with gloves. I still could not remember taking them off or what I had done with them. I eventually dug down about eight or ten inches and found nothing. It was just as dry at that level as it had been at the surface. I gave the idea up.

It was late afternoon now, and I had been on the ground for more than 24 hours. That was just a guess; I didn't know how long. I still had no water. I was hungry and sore. I was not in any pain, just really sore like the day after a car wreck. Still blind in the left eye.

My good friend Apache 16 (Bob Smith) had been shot down a few days before. He had been brought down with small arms fire; and upon crashing, his aircraft did a complete end over end flip into the bamboo. Everyone got out all right; the C & C bird came in immediately and picked them up. Smitty figured his total time on the ground after the crash was maybe five minutes. Why couldn't my crash have been like that?

I wondered what 16 thought about all this. I knew if he thought that there was any chance of us being alive he would be out here looking for us. All of Apache would be out here looking for us if they thought there was any chance at all. I wondered if Apache 14 (Bob Spencer) had heard anything about this. He was in the hospital with malaria, the lucky shit.

I followed the twisting dry streambed for the next 30 to 40 minutes. It turned back and forth like any creek, but overall it was running south to southeast. I finally saw something ahead of me a few yards lying in the creek bed. I thought at first that it was a dead animal; it looked dark in the distance, and I could not see very well. It was not a dead animal but I could not quite make it out until I was on top of it.

It was water. It was water! A very shallow elongated puddle of water about two feet long almost like you would find in a tire track. I could not believe it, but there it was. A small stagnant pool, covered with slime and insects. The slim and the bugs did not matter; it was water and it was mine. I looked farther down the stream, and there was another one; this one was a little longer and deeper. I hurried over to it; it was in the same shape as the first one, stagnant slime and bugs. I didn't care.

I pushed aside the gunk and water spiders with my hands and cleared a small place on the surface of the water. Then I got my first drink of water since the day before when I had stepped in the hole crossing the river. I gorged myself on as much water as I could possibly drink and then vomited. It was not because of what the water looked like or smelled like; it was simply the fact that I had completely stuffed myself, and I was not used to that amount of water. I lost everything I had taken in. I wiped off my mouth on my sleeve and then drank from the pool until I was completely full again. This time I kept it down, but I was so bloated that I could barely move. I sat down on the edge of the bank and thanked God for the water.

It was now late afternoon, and would be getting dark quickly. I hated to leave my newfound water, but I needed to keep moving. It was obvious that I was not going to be picked up today. I would be spending another night in the jungle; I just hoped I would be alone. I needed to find someplace like the thicket of thorns that had protected me the night before, somewhere I could conceal myself and sleep with some sense of invisibility and security.

I needed something to carry water in, and I had nothing. The best I could do was stuff myself until I could not hold another drop and hope that I would find water again soon. I checked to make sure I had not left tracks around the pool of water or anything else to show that I had been there. There wasn't anything I could do about the vomit. It was all water anyway; it would dry soon. I took another long drink from the pool, and like saying goodbye to an old friend, walked away and did not look back.

I walked quietly for a few minutes and continued to follow the dried up stream. The ravine became deeper as I walked, and it occurred to me that I should probably now be walking on the high ground above the creek. I climbed up the steep slope trying not to leave boot marks.

It was very difficult to walk without making noise. The entire area I had come through since finding my way out of the maze was covered in dry leaves. They were everywhere, including the streambed. Whatever these trees were, they apparently shed leaves part of the year. I knew I was making too much damn noise.

I decided it was too difficult to try to move along the top of the ravine and opted to drop back down into the bed where the walking was easier and much quieter. I walked slowly and tried to be as silent as I could be. I was 50 to 75 meters from the pool of water when I noticed well above the ravine two trees growing closely together. I climbed back out of the ravine to take a look at them. They appeared to be what I had been looking for.

Each tree was roughly two feet in diameter, and their bases were very close together. From a distance, especially at the bottom of the ravine, they almost looked like two trunks coming out of the same tree. However, they were separate trees, and as their trunks grew towards the sun, they also grew farther apart giving the appearance of a large "V" shape. The trees were a few feet back from the edge of the ravine, which at this point was probably eight to ten feet deep. A position from behind the trees looking through the "V" commanded a view up and down the stream. Someone walking down the streambed would never see me hiding there unless they came up to look.

To my rear were small trees and bushes that would also hide me reasonably well after it was dark. It was a good defensive position. It would have to be; it was getting dark fast. Once again, I wished I had my M-16.

I made myself a bed of leaves, hoping I could make the hard ground a little more comfortable and decided to make one more trip back to my pool of water. I slipped back down into the ravine and stuck a large stick in the ground in the middle of the streambed abeam of my hiding place above. I hoped when I came back in the quickly failing light I would be able to find the stick and then my hiding place. I listened carefully to the jungle; and hearing nothing, I hurried back to the pool of water as quickly and as quietly as I could.

I drank until I could not hold anymore. My trips to the water were beginning to leave marks around the area. I hid my footprints with some leaves and hurried back to find my stick. I pulled the stick out of the ground and tossed it to the side as I made my way up the steep slope to my new hideout.

I sat with my back to the small trees and bushes and gazed through the "V" to the emptiness below. I saw nothing. It was now very dark. The entire NVA could have been in the ravine, and I would not have been able to see them. But I was confident that they would not be able to see me either. I sat in absolute silence and listened. There was nothing.

I told myself that the longer I was able to avoid capture, the more likely it was that I would *not be* captured. I was not sure that was true, but it *was* true that if I had been pursued or followed, they would have found me and taken me by now. If the NVA were able to figure out that I was not on the bottom of the river with the wreckage of the aircraft, they would have been "beating the bushes" to find me. That meant they had either decided that I had died in the crash or that they had been driven off by the battle that followed. Either scenario was good for me.

I felt that every hour and every mile I was able to put between myself and the area of the crash was in my favor. If they found me now, it would be because I did something stupid and let myself get caught. If they knew I was not dead, they had put the word out to all their units to be looking for me. It would no longer be the original guys who shot me down who would find me now; it would be some other unit that knew about it. The most important advantages that I had were silence and darkness. It would be easier for me to stay in one place perfectly still and make no noise than it would be for them to be quiet if they were moving at night.

I wondered if it was possible I had traveled far enough south that there were no enemy units between me and Snuol. I supposed that was too much to ask for. Almost all of that firing the day before had seemed to come from the north side of the river. I did not have any idea how far I had come from the crash. I had spent so much of the first day moving west and then trying to get through the maze that I probably had not traveled south more than the length of a football field. I realized that with all the twisting and turning I might only be a few hundred yards from the original crash site. That was a depressing thought.

I had to continue the assumption that I was surrounded by the NVA and that we had no "friendlies" on the ground. This was still no "walk in the woods." It was a long way to Snuol, and I believed the possibility of making it there without being captured was still nonexistent. I lowered the hammer on my .38, so it would not be cocked if I accidently rolled over on it in my sleep. I did not need the noise of accidental discharge or the possibility of shooting myself. I curled up on my bed of leaves and laid the revolver down close beside me. I continued to lie silently and listen to the jungle until I fell asleep.

Chapter Eleven

My 30-day leave seemed as if it only lasted a week. My mother and my grandmother were thrilled to see me, my friends seemed happy to see me, but everything was different now. No one had any idea where I had been or what I had seen, and I had not even been to war yet. Kunkel's Drive In in Connersville was still the same, the same kids cruising through on Friday and Saturday nights. Nothing had changed for them.

I left from Dayton, Ohio (roughly an hour's drive from my grandmother's home in Richmond, Indiana) on a commercial flight to the east coast to meet a military contract flight to the west coast. Did not seem to make sense to me, but there you go. From McGuire Air Force Base (across the road from Ft. Dix, New Jersey), we flew to Seattle, Washington. From there we flew to Anchorage, Alaska. This time we were only on the ground for an hour. It was daylight now and I spent most of the time looking out the airport gift shop windows at the beautiful mountains. No time to leave the building.

Next stop -- Yokota, Japan, twenty some miles northwest of Tokyo. Another refuel stop, take on more food, take off the trash, clean and refill the restrooms, and a much needed chance for us to stretch our legs. Even for me, a short guy, the seats were cramped. The airlines had the seats much closer together for military contract flights than they did for regular commercial passengers. Once again, no time to look around or leave the base. I did get to see Mt. Fuji before we landed. Next stop -- South Vietnam.

We landed at Long Binh Air Base, which, I was to find out, was about half way between Saigon and Bien Hoa. We were bused from there to Bien Hoa, one of the largest, if not the largest, United States Air Force bases in South Vietnam. It was also home to several United States Army units. The Air Force was on one side of the complex, and the Army was on the other. It was also the location of the REPO DEPO (Replacement Center) where all incoming Army personnel (in the southern part of South Vietnam) were housed while they figured out what to do with us. We would be here for the next three or four days while they decided where we were going, what units we would be assigned to based on our MOS (Military Occupational Specialty/our jobs) determined by our training.

I knew almost nothing about the various combat units in Vietnam, who had their own aviation and who did not. We filled out a "dream sheet," selecting our first, second, and third choices of divisions -- not that the Army actually ever went by what you requested. I put down the First Air Cavalry Division (Airmobile) as my first choice. I knew nothing about it, but I did like the look of the 1st Air Cavalry Division patch, the largest in the Army. It was a large yellow sort of triangular-shaped patch with a black horse's head in the top right corner and a black diagonal stripe.

I met a second tour aviator who tried to give me some advice,

"You don't want assigned to any cavalry unit," he said.

"Why not?" I asked.

"Because, pal, you want to live through this tour and go home. Stay away from the CAV, especially the 1st Cav. And if you do get assigned to the 1st Air Cav, for God's sake's, don't get assigned to the First of the Ninth."

"What's that," I said, not telling him that I had already put down the 1st Air Cav as my first choice on my dream sheet.

"It's a cavalry squadron in the 1st Air Cav. They have Hueys, gunships, and scout birds. They also have their own internal infantry platoons. They are always into something. What do you know about the Battle of the Ia Drang in '65?"

"Nothing," I said, with a blank look.

"You're shitting me!"

"No, really, I don't know anything about it."

"And how long have you been in the Army?"

"Fourteen months."

"Damn, well, anyway, it was a big-ass battle in the Ia Drang Valley back in 1965 shortly after the 1st Air Cav arrived in country. The first time a large American unit fought against the regular NVA, the North Vietnamese Army. You do know who they are, right?"

"Yes, Chief."

"Any way, long story short, that whole battle started with the 1st of the 9th finding what appeared to be a large enemy force. You gotta read more, son."

"Right."

He spoke to me as if I were his grandson. He was probably only two or three years older than I was, but he was a Huey pilot, a second-tour aviator, and a CW2 (Chief Warrant Officer 2). I wondered where *he* was going.

Within a couple of days I was assigned to the 1st Air Cavalry Division. We had all of our patches sewn on right there at the Replacement Center by local Vietnamese seamstresses who worked there on the base. I wondered about that; I thought we were not supposed to trust any Vietnamese, and here they were right here on post. They had to be off the compound by 16:00. (4:00 pm).

I did not have any flight suits yet; they were to be issued once we arrived at division, so all of the patches I had paid to be sewn on (out of my own pocket, I was an officer now) were on "jungle fatigues" that I would never wear again. They were brand new rip-stop olive drab jungle fatigues, what everyone else in the Army was wearing, unless you were in aviation. Then you had to wear the new two-piece fire resistant nomex flight suit. Fire resistant, NOT fire proof. That change had recently happened in the Army: no more cotton one-piece coverall type flight suits, and no more flying in jungle fatigues.

The same with "jungle boots." I was issued three pair of those, but I could not legally fly in them as a pilot or a crewmember because, although the lower part of the boot was leather with rubber soles, the upper part around your ankle was nylon, which in the case of an aircraft fire, would melt into your ankles and could not be easily removed. The Army knew, and we knew, that if you crashed, you burned; it was automatic.

They had taken all of our American cash, coins as well as paper, from us when we first arrived, so I was trying to get used to using MPC (Military Pay Certificates). It reminded me of monopoly money printed in various colors with astronauts and ships and planes on it. They were printed in $1, $5, $10, and $20 denominations, but they were also printed in 5, 10, 25, and 50 cent notes. There were no coins.

On my fourth day "in country," I was transferred to the 1st Air Cavalry Division. Division "rear" was stationed right here in Bien Hoa not far from the REPO DEPO. A small group of us were taken over there where we would stay for another four or five days while division once again decided where we were going and what units within the 1st Cav we would be assigned to. More paper work, more waiting. We all wanted to finally be assigned to somebody and try to settle in somewhere.

During the days at division rear we were all required to go through several classes of the 1st Air Cavalry Division's version of "in country orientation." Some classes I actually considered useful, some not so much. Of course, I really did not know anything about anything, so most of it was new to me. I listened.

On the 25th of August we were all bused outside the "green line" (the berm, the protective bunker complex around the compound) to a set of bleachers overlooking a large open field. The outside classroom setup was very similar to Army classes I had had at Ft. Polk. The bleachers were covered by a high roof that gave us shade and allowed for a breeze, although the air was still very hot.

This morning's class would be on how to call in ARA (Aerial Rocket Artillery). No different really from calling in conventional ground artillery, except aerial rocket artillery was fired by helicopters, either Hueys modified for that purpose or Cobra gunships.

There were still some B Model Huey gunships in country and some Charlie and Mike models around, but those were all variations of the UH-1 utility helicopter. Most had now been replaced by the AH-1G Cobra gunship, which was built from the ground up to be a gunship. The others were really field modifications of "utility" helicopters. It had a very narrow cockpit compared to a Huey, with one pilot sitting behind the other, and therefore presented a much narrower target to the enemy when attacking in a gun run.

Today's class and demonstration would be put on by the impressive and well known 2nd Battalion of the 20th Artillery, ARA. They had two of their Cobras out there, and the idea was to show us that anyone could call in aerial artillery if they had a radio and the right frequency. The instructors for this class were two of the 2/20th pilots wearing their black ball caps signifying that they were "Gun" pilots. They were talking to their aircraft on an FM radio with large speakers, so we could hear what they were saying to each other.

The demonstration went well; they did not actually fire any rockets, and we were getting ready to leave the bleachers for the bus. The two Cobras were kind of playing around with each other like an aerial dog fight with both of them making gun runs on the bleachers. First one low dive and pass, then another, but this time the second one did not pull out in time. You could see the nose of the aircraft pitched up for the pullout, but the aircraft "mushed" through the hot thin air and crashed into the ground belly first with the nose still raised. We were all stunned.

There was a huge explosion of JP-4 jet fuel. We could all feel the heat from the explosion and now the fire. We were in shock. Holy shit, is this for real!? We all just stared out at the open field with our mouths open. The burning wreckage was probably about 100 yards from us, about the length of a football field; we were in no danger. I started running towards the burning aircraft, well, there really wasn't any aircraft, but I started running to the fire. Someone was yelling, "Stay back, stay back, everyone stay back!" I knew no one could have lived through that, but I was not going to just stand there. Those were fellow Army aviators.

I reached what was left of the aircraft and looked for survivors, bodies, anything that looked like a human being, but there wasn't anything. I finally concentrated on the largest piece, other than the engine and rotor blades, and realized that that was what was left of a person. It was a body, really only a torso, still strapped into a seat. Hands and arms gone, legs and feet gone, no face, and still on fire. I was not in a flight suit and, of course, had no nomex flight gloves, But I began to tamp out the fire on the body with my bare hands. Eventually someone brought me a blanket to throw over the body and I continued to tamp out the fire until it was out.

Someone had called MEDEVAC, and a Huey arrived. Soon there were medics everywhere and fire trucks. But the pilots were gone, gone for good, in seconds. One fatal mistake, not even in combat, just a terrible accident. I needed to wash my hands.

I found out later that the pilots were both warrants, one a CW2, probably close to the end of his tour, and the other, a WO1. I thought out loud, "What a waste, what a tragic waste!" Being shot down in combat was one thing, but this, how do you explain this accident to the families? I wondered if they would be told the details. Probably not, what good would it do? I thought the families would decide their loved ones died in the Vietnam War, accident or combat, did it really make any difference?

Apache Troop pilot's hootches. The TOC on the left, Song Be Mountain (Nui Ba Ra) in the distance. 1970 My Photo

My end of the "SHEY' boys hootch. Bob Spencer, Max Evans, and I lived here for seven months

Twenty year old WO1 Craig (Jeff) Houser Song Be 1970 My Photo

The author with his collection of weapons: top to bottom; his issued American M-16, and two AK-47s that he traded for. Song Be 1970 My Photo

The author in his hootch with his folding-stock AK-47. It was short enough that if fit nicely in the front of the OH-6 LOH. Song Be 1970

The author having recently received the Distinguished Flying Cross Song Be 1970 My Photo

WO1 Bob Spencer and WO1 Craig (Jeff) Houser popping Jiffy Pop over a 105 mm shell casing. Song Be 1970 My Photo

The author and 1Lt Max Evans sharing popcorn in our hootch. Song Be 1970

WO1 Craig (Jeff) Houser and his assigned LOH OH-6A #67-16273.
Song Be 1970

WO1 Bob Smith (Apache 16) Song Be 1971 My Photo

1Lt Max Evans (Apache 38) Song Be 1971

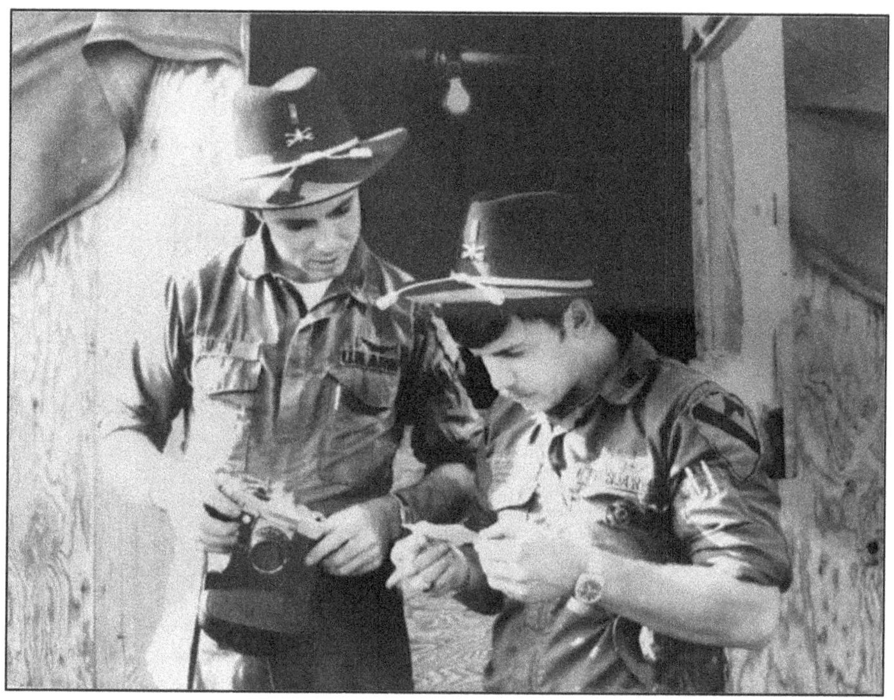

WO1 Bob Smith (Apache 16) and the author on the right. Notice the "Crash Bracelet" on my right wrist and the new Seiko watch on my left wrist. Song Be 1971 My Photo

Cpt James Kurtz (Apache Red) Phuoc Vinh 1971

Cpt Tom Agness (Apache 36) lounging between missions in the shade of the rubber trees. Loc Ninh 1971 My Photo

WO1 Bob Spencer (Apache 14) Playing cards in the rubber trees with several ARVN (the Browns) soldiers watching. Loc Ninh 1971

(L to R) WO1 Bob Spencer, Cpt Max Evans, CW2 Stanley McCaw, 1Lt Gilbert Medina, Cpt John Liberg. Phuoh Vinh 1971

WO1 Craig (Jeff) Houser (Apache 12) being hugged and helped By Cpt James Kurtz (Apache Red) to the waiting Huey flown by AC Cpt Max Evans (Apache 38) and Cpt Tom Agness (Apache 36) Snuol, Cambodia March 1971 Max Evans Photo

Ralph shared our hootch with the three us when I served as Liaison Officer with the ARVNs. Di An 1971

Author with burns healing, eyes getting better, new watch. Di An 1971 My Photo

WO1 Bob Spencer with a Headhunter Huey Phuoc Vinh 1971

WO1 Bob Spencer (Apache 14) Phuoc Vinh 1971

My Seiko watch ripped from my wrist in the crash and lost 10 March 1971 in Cambodia. Recovered by JPAC on the bottom of the river 5 February 2005 34 years later! My Photo

Now Col James Kurtz (Ret) and the author standing in front of Panel 4 West of the Vietnam Veterans Memorial Wall, Washington, D.C. 2008 My Photo

Max Evans flying Skycranes Erickson Heavy Lift. 2017 My Photo

Tom Agness 2004. Now LTC Tom Agness (Ret) My Photo

Chapter Twelve

Division had decided that I would now go to 1st of the 9th, the First Squadron of the 9th Cavalry Regiment. The squadron headquarters was located in Phuoc Vinh, wherever that was. I was driven in a jeep to the base of the control tower at the airstrip and told to get on a Chinook, a CH-47 heavy-lift helicopter. There were a bunch of people standing there, and most of them looked as lost as I was.

"You look lost, Chief," said an older sergeant sitting on his pack at the base of the tower.

"I am lost," I said.

"I was not used to being called "chief," and it kind of threw me. I took it as a sign of respect, but I was not actually a "chief"; you were not a Chief Warrant Officer until you were a CW2 or above. It went up to CW4. I had never seen a CW3 or CW4, but I knew they were out there somewhere.

"Where you headin'?"

"Phuoc Vinh," I said, looking at the red dust that swirled everywhere from the 47's rotor wash even though he was still at flight idle. It would be much worse when he lifted off.

"I think that's your ride right there, Sir," said the sergeant, motioning to the Chinook. "But you probably better ask the guys in the tower; they'll know."

"Thank you," I said, and started to climb up the tower steps. Just then one of the operators in the tower hung over the railing and yelled to us that anyone headed for Phuoc Vinh should get on that bird, as he pointed to the Chinook. I said goodbye to the sergeant, who was apparently not going with us, and walked over to the CH-47. The rear cargo ramp was already down, and the inside was filling up fast. I yelled to the crew chief and asked if this bird was going to Phuoc Vinh, and he nodded his head.

I had a brand new flight suit on, and it made me look brand new, which, of course, I was. I would have gladly worn an old used one if supply had had it. I had nomex flight gloves now and all leather boots but still no helmet that would have to be issued by troop. No ear plugs, no ear protection of any kind. That was my first time sitting in the back of a Chinook, and I hoped the last. The engines and transmissions screamed loudly as if they were in pain; oil or transmission fluid, probably both, leaked all down the inside wall of the cargo compartment. I pointed out the leaks to the crew chief, and he just nodded his head. Once we took off all the sounds were worse, with the aircraft bouncing and slipping from side to side. I thought, "God, let me out of this thing." This cannot be the way guys feel in the back of a Huey; they love to ride in Hueys.

Phuoc Vinh was located due north of Bien Hoa about 20 miles so the flight did not take long at all, and I was more than glad to be back on the ground. They let us out in the vicinity of the tower, but as with Bien Hoa, the pilots were careful not to get too close to the other parked aircraft. The rotor wash from a Chinook at full operating RPM is tremendous. I gathered my bags and walked over to the base of the tower. It was then I noticed that I was not the only guy in a nice new flight suit. There were others, and one had a face I recognized: Tommy Pepper, a classmate of mine at Ft. Wolters. I yelled to him.

We talked a few minutes and were soon joined by two other WO1s. We got directions to squadron headquarters and started walking that way lugging our bags.

Squadron headquarters was located in an old yellow French stucco building just off the road that bordered the airstrip. There was a Huey main rotor blade planted vertically in a concrete mound in the middle of the courtyard in front of the building. The rotor blade was painted red and white, the colors of the cavalry, and painted on the blade in block letters were all the campaigns that the 1st of the 9th had ever been involved in. Not just in Vietnam, but also in World War II and Korea. Surrounding the mound were enemy weapons that had been seized in various operations including Cambodia back in May and June of 1970.

We met the XO, and he welcomed us to the "CAV" and especially to the 1st of the 9th. He explained that although Headquarters Troop and Charlie Troop were located here at Phuoc Vinh, the other Air Cav troops were spread out in other locations: Alpha Troop was farther north at Song Be, Bravo Troop was southeast of Bien Hoa at Bearcat, and Echo Troop was southwest of here at Lai Khe. Of course, I did not know where any of these places were, but I listened and tried to remember. Delta Troop was located here but had no aviation assets; it consisted of all ground vehicles that patrolled the roads mainly at night with jeeps and other heavily armed vehicles. They reminded me of a TV show I used to watch called *The Rat Patrol,* and that is what they called themselves.

Then, out of nowhere, the major said, "Gentlemen, we need Scout Pilots. I know you all came out of Rucker as Huey pilots, but what we really need are Scouts. It's all volunteer, but that's what we need. Who wants to volunteer?"

I was young, dumb, and single, and I had a TAC officer at Ft. Wolters that I really liked who had been a Scout Pilot in Vietnam flying OH-6s. He had pictures of LOHs (Low Observation Helicopters pronounced loaches) all over his office walls. I had really admired him; maybe this was something I would like to do?

I looked over at Tommy, and he looked at me. We were apparently both thinking the same thing. We both told the major that we would volunteer. Then one of the others said that he would also. The fourth "newbie" was reluctant. He was married and said that he preferred to stay in Hueys. The major said that was fine and thanked us.

I was assigned to Troop A, Alpha Troop, more commonly referred to as Apache Troop. I would be going to Song Be. Tommy Pepper would be going to Troop C, Charlie Troop, right here in Phuoc Vinh. The third new Scout would go to Troop E, Echo Troop, in Lai Khe. The fourth guy would be assigned to Headquarters Troop right here in Phuoc Vinh and stay in Hueys. We were told where the mess hall and the club were and to get something to eat while they figured out transportation for the two of us who would be moving on.

While Tommy and I were talking at "Pinetree," the Charlie Troop and Headquarters Troop parking area of revetments, I noticed a Huey with yellow crossed sabers and the 1st of the 9th painted on the nose. All the Hueys here had that, but this one was different. Charlie Troop aircraft had a yellow circle painted on their doors, but this one had a distinctive yellow triangle on its doors. It also had "Headhunters" painted on the nose along with the crossed sabers. Only Apache Troop Hueys were The Headhunters. This might be my ride.

Tommy and I decided to get a look at the club, so still dragging all of our luggage, we headed that way. Later that day I was told there would be an Apache Troop Huey leaving that afternoon for Song Be and not to miss it.

Turned out that was my ride. I walked up to the Huey while the crew was getting ready to take off. They had not cranked yet, and I asked one of the pilots if they were going to Song Be. He said that they were and to go ahead and grab a seat. I had already said goodbye and good luck to Tommy and the other guys; they were looking for a place to stay. I still had no helmet, but a crew chief handed me an extra headset so I had hearing protection and could listen to the pilots make their radio calls and talk to each other and their crew. We eased out of Pinetree and our hover to the north became a takeoff.

We skimmed over the 105 mm artillery pieces; Phuoc Vinh was, after all, among other things a FSB (Fire Support Base) We crossed the Greenline and the endless strands of concertina barbed wire and continued to climb north. Song Be was another 40 miles or so north of

Phuoc Vinh; we kept getting closer and closer to the Cambodian border, something I really did not think much about at the time.

The terrain continued to change, and the elevation was increasing. Between Bien Hoa and Phuoc Vinh, there had been a lot of rice paddies on both sides of the Dong Nai River, but the closer we got to Phuoc Vinh, the rice paddies became fewer and fewer, and now there were none. The paddies had now become forests, maybe not quite jungle, but somewhere in between. There were lakes and rivers and some open areas, but no rice paddies. I would later learn that there was actually a lot of rice down there, but it was not in paddies; it was "highland rice" planted in small fields often on the sides of hills, not in water.

The terrain between Phuoc Vinh and Song Be continued to change, more forests or jungle, hills, a lot of bamboo. We had been following the road north out of Phuoc Vinh. About halfway there at a place called Dong Xoai, the road forked with one road headed off to the northeast and the other headed north northwest. From here, in daylight and good weather, you could clearly see Nui Ba Ra, the one and only mountain at Song Be. Actually, the one and only mountain anywhere around for miles. It rose above the jungle like an upside down ice-cream cone.

North of the mountain lay the town of Song Be, not a village but an actual town. In days past tourists from farther south used to come up here. Not anymore. About three miles west of the mountain was FSB Buttons, what *we* all referred to as Song Be or Song Be Base Camp. This was going to be my home.

Part III

12 March 1971

Day Three

Chapter Thirteen

I slowly came out of my sleep. I tried to focus not just my eyes but also my mind. It took me a moment to remember where I was and how I had gotten there. I thought it was probably eight or nine o'clock. The jungle was quiet. I could not understand why there was no noise, none at all.

I knew from hunting squirrels when I was a kid back in Indiana that when you first walk into a woods, all the animals hear you and become absolutely silent. I learned from my dad that the best thing to do was to find a place to sit down and be quiet for 15 or 20 minutes, and the woods would come back to life. I usually sat down against a tree trunk on those very early mornings and fell asleep.

But why was the jungle so quiet now? I had not made any noise in hours, not since I went to sleep last night. Did that mean that I made noise in my sleep or that someone was here with me? I was thirsty, but I decided to stay where I was for a while. I peered through the "V" in the two trees to the ravine below and listened to the jungle. There was no movement, no sounds, just silence.

I remained motionless and quiet for roughly an hour, and then I decided to make my way back to the pool of water one last time. I pulled my .38 out of its holster and cocked it. I walked slowly and quietly back to the water, trying to be silent but knowing that was almost impossible in the leaves. I checked my vision again as I walked and found there was little change from the day before. Some light was entering my left eye, but it was still useless, and near vision was very blurry out of my right eye. Distance vision with the right was not too bad, but I still had to tilt my head to the left and rearward almost to the point that it actually hurt just to be able to look through the bottom of my eye.

I drank as much as I could hold without making myself sick and wondered when I would be able to drink again. I had already determined that I had to move on. I brushed some leaves over the area where I had knelt down to drink; I could not see any signs that I had been drinking there, and I hoped that no one else would be able to either. I left the water and headed back toward my den.

It was difficult to leave the water that I had had so much trouble finding. I came to the point in the streambed that lay below the hiding place where I had spent the night. It was very tempting to stay there a while longer where I had water and relative safety. I fought a battle in my own mind whether to stay or leave. I knew I could not stay. What could I gain from that? I had to keep moving.

I followed the ravine for the next half an hour or so. It meandered back and forth, but generally it had been taking me southeast. It was now beginning to take me more to the west. I stayed with it for a few more minutes to see if it would return to my course, but it did not. I also did not find any more water in it. I retraced my steps back to a prominent bend I had walked through earlier and decided that would be the point where I left the stream. I walked up out of the streambed, took a bearing on my compass, and looked off to the southeast.

The jungle was more like a forest now with more and more light penetrating through the canopy above. I walked a few paces and almost immediately came upon a trail. It seemed to be heading southeast, so I followed it.

My morale was the highest it had been since before the crash. I had more confidence now for some reason. I continued to tell myself that it was now March the 12th; it had been two days since I had been shot down -- two days and two nights. This was now my third day in the jungle. I had not been captured or killed immediately as I had thought I would be. I had not been captured traveling in the daytime, which was almost guaranteed. I had survived two days now without being caught, and I had found water. There was hope. I began to actually consider the possibility that I might be able to avoid capture and make it all the way to Snuol. More importantly, not only did I consider the possibility, I began to believe it myself.

The trail came upon a dry stream and crossed it. I walked down the streambed about 25 yards and did not find any sign of water, so I retraced my steps until I came back to the trail and decided to go upstream. That also proved futile, so I returned to the trail and continued to follow it until it began to turn more and more to the west. I left the trail and headed out cross-country on my south-southeast course. It did not take long until I found another trail, which I followed until it too began to turn too much to the west for me, and at that point I left it to stay on my course.

I spent several hours repeating the process of walking trails until they turned the wrong way and leaving them until I found another. I came across several tributaries, and all of them were dry. I decided it was time to take a break, so I left the trail and sat behind some trees to rest and think. It was hot; this morning's last drink of water was only a memory. I had to have water, and I prayed to God for it.

While I rested, I sat cross-legged with my feet drawn up close to me and noticed the terrible shape my boots were in. Walking and crawling through the weeds and vines had taken a heavy toll on what had been a decent shine. The toes were now down to raw leather. I thought to myself how those boots would have been worth about a million demerits back in flight school at Ft. Wolters or Ft. Rucker. However, that was a hundred years ago, and I did not shine my boots anymore; we paid hootch maids to do that.

Back at Song Be we had paid our hootch maid five dollars a month to wash our clothes, shine our boots, and straighten up and sweep out the hootch. She received five bucks from each of the four of us in the hootch and she was probably working for another six or eight guys, so she was making 50 or 60 dollars a month, and we paid her in MPC, not Vietnamese piasters. That was a lot of money for those girls for "honest" work. The only Vietnamese who made more than that were either selling drugs or themselves.

As I sat looking at my boots, I noticed a distinctive "V" shaped cut on the toe of my right boot. "I'll be damned," I said to myself almost out loud. That cut had not come from the jungle; I had done that myself back at Ft. Wolters, Texas, the first week that I had been there. We had been placed in "Snowbirds," a holding company for newly arrived candidates, waiting their turn to be assigned to one of the ten warrant officer candidate companies "up on the hill."

The wait in Snowbirds could be several weeks and the TAC Officers had to be creative to keep us busy. On that particular day they had us mowing and weeding around the barracks. I had been using a spade-like device with a blade on it to cut the grass along the edge of a sidewalk. During the course of the afternoon, I had missed and cut the toe of my boot not once but twice with the damn thing. I had learned all the tricks of putting a good "spit shine" on a pair of boots while I was in basic training, but those two cuts had given me fits for months both at Ft. Wolters and Ft. Rucker. I had eventually found that I could fill in the cuts with hot Kiwi boot polish. I built the polish base up over a period of time until you could no longer tell there was any damage there. I had not seen those cuts since Texas. "Texas, so long ago," I thought to myself.

I had loved being stationed in Texas. The country was beautiful, and the people were friendly. I daydreamed about flying the TH-55 solo over the prairies of north central Texas and landing on mesas in what seemed to be the middle of nowhere. Now I knew what "nowhere" *really* meant. I had rested long enough; I needed to get moving. I had to find water.

I stepped back out on the trail and took another bearing on my compass. The trail seemed to be running close to south-southeast; it would work for now. As I walked, my thoughts turned to Kiser and Smoot. I wondered if they had also made it out of the crash. Maybe they were out here somewhere with me, trying to get back. Maybe they had already been picked up and rescued. I knew the odds were that they were dead, or worse.

I still could not believe I had lived through the crash. That should have killed me. Then I should have drowned in the river, and almost did. I did not know why or how I had survived those events, but it was hard to believe that anyone else had. How could that be possible? The fact that one of us was alive must have been a "one in a million" chance. On the other hand, *I was alive*, maybe they were too.

We took the hit on the right side in the area of the engine compartment. We were burning on the way down. It occurred to me that sitting back there, Smoot might have been blown out of the aircraft with the initial impact. Or, he may have decided to jump out of the burning aircraft while we were over the river. In either case, he would not have been in the aircraft on the bottom of the river with me, which could account for me not seeing him when I came to the surface and when I crawled up the bank and out of the river.

But what about Kiser? He was right next to me, literally inches away. What had happened to Kiser? I made it out; he could have made it out.

While I was thinking about Kiser and Smoot, the trail had turned to the west, and I had not realized it. "Shit," I said, under my breath. I had to pay more attention and not daydream. I could retrace my steps and fix this, but what if I had stepped on a "booby trap" in the trail or walked into a trap. I could not let my guard down and become complacent I told myself. I turned around and walked back 20 yards to where the gentle turn to the west had started. I left the trail and traveled though sparse trees until I found another trail. That trail did not work long for me either, so I abandoned that one to stay on my course.

The walking was not difficult here; the area was mainly sparse trees and deep grass. The canopy overhead cut out much of the light, but I had plenty enough to see. I had been walking roughly two hours since the last stop, and I thought it was about time to take another break. I was about to do that when I realized that something was out of place ahead of me. I was not on a trail at the time, and I was almost on top of it before I saw it. It was a hootch! If it was occupied, I had walked right into a trap.

I stood completely still for a very long time and then slowly knelt down on one knee. There was no sound; there was no movement. I had to decide whether to try to quietly backtrack and try to get away, or go ahead and walk up to it. I did not smell any rice cooking, and there were no other signs of life. I decided to investigate and hoped that I would find water or food or both. Even if there was not any water, maybe I would at least find something to carry it in the next time I found it. I walked very quietly up to the hootch with my revolver drawn and cocked.

There was no sign of life. The hootch had been there for some time, and it was not occupied. It was about nine or ten feet wide by about 12 or 14 feet long. The "walls" of the hootch were not walls at all. What had appeared to me from a distance to be walls were actually heavy rectangular burlap bags stacked one on top of the other until they were above my head. Bamboo poles held up a "roof" that just barely covered the bags. The bags and the roof were carefully camouflaged.

I slowly walked though a gap between the burlap bags that apparently served as an entrance, and looked at one of the bags piled next to me. It had a small hole in one corner, and rice had been leaking out on the ground. This was not a hootch at all; this was a rich cache!

"I'll be a son of a bitch," I thought to myself. "I've walked right up on a rice cache!"

Those bags were at least two 200 pounds each, and there were at least 20 bags, maybe more. How much was that? I was never any good at math. Twenty bags at 200 pounds a bag. Damn, that was 4000 fucking pounds of rice! That was literally enough to feed a small army, and that was exactly what they intended to do with it.

Where did they get all this rice? How the hell did they move all of these bags here? I didn't think you could carry those on bicycles? I didn't know. You would think that you would have to use trucks to carry bags that size…or elephants. Trucks would not fit on any of these trails I had been on, and there was no indication of elephants. I did not see any elephant tracks or any of the large smashed down areas in the grass where they lay down. On the other hand, this had been here for a long time. During the rainy season, the tracks and the elephant dung would be washed away, and the grass would grow back. I reached in the hole in the sack and scooped out a handful of the rice. I put some in my mouth and tried to eat it. It was too hard; it was like chewing on small gravel. I would have to cook it to eat it, and that meant a fire and smoke. I was not willing to take that chance; at least not yet. I wanted to destroy it, but I did not have anything to destroy it with. A few cartridges of stink gas from an M-79 would be good right now. I could not very well burn it with my Zippo, and even if I could, I did not want to let the enemy know I was here. Damn, I hated to leave it!

There was no other food or water in the cache: no pots or pans, nothing to cook with, nothing to carry water in. The trails around it had not had any use for quite some time. The hootch was not a hootch at all. This place was not for living or hiding out; this was a supply depot hidden away for NVA forces to use when they were working in this area. I was sure there were dozens, if not hundreds, of these caches out here. I would remember this and turn it in if I ever got back. However,

I knew I would never be able to pinpoint it on a map. Hell, I did not have a clue where I was. I did not have the means to destroy it or booby trap it, and I would never be able to tell anyone where I had found it. I had to leave it for the NVA in the same condition that I had found it. Damn.

I walked out the other end of the cache, took one last look at it, and returned to my south-southeast course. I needed water. Why had I not found the river? This was now the third day, so I should have found the river by now. I was reasonably sure I had not been traveling in circles; after traveling largely westerly the first day, I had tried to keep a good south-southeast compass course. I had done that for two days. The only explanation had to be that the river I had crashed in and then later crossed was the river I had been looking for. I must have crashed farther south than I realized. My plan had been to find the river and then follow it east to the bombed out bridge. That would put me on Highway 13.

OK, so if I was already south of the river, and I had been traveling all this time, then I had to be farther south than I thought. Did that make sense? That meant that if I continued this course I would eventually hit the highway, but much farther south than I had thought. I wished I had someone else to discuss all this with and get a "sanity check."

The sparse trees ahead of me were thinning out. There was a lot of light up ahead. It was a clearing, and I approached cautiously. I sat inside the tree line and looked at what had been at one time a rice paddy. It had long since dried up, and I did not think it had been used for years. The sun was hot, and the light was blinding. My one "good" eye had become used to the heavily shaded protection of the jungle. I waited for my right eye to adjust to the light while I tried to decide whether to cross the open area or go around it. It looked like it was probably 40 or 50 yards across the clearing to the tree line on the other side. In those few moments it would take me to cover that distance, I would be completely out in the open.

I considered staying in the trees until it was dark and then crossing the rice paddy. However, darkness would not come to the clearing for several hours. I still had no water; I had not had anything to drink since that morning. I had to find water while I still had daylight. I also did not want to enter the tree line on the other side in total darkness. I needed to find water and a place to stay for the night while I could still see.

I thought about staying inside the tree line of the jungle and going around the clearing, but that seemed like such a huge waste of time. I could be across the open field and in the trees on the other side in minutes, or I could spend another two hours going around it. How would I mark my position so that I would know when I was directly across the field from where I was now? There were no distinguishing landmarks in the opposite tree line. I decided to go ahead and chance it. This could turn out to be a very foolish mistake.

I did not run; I was not sure that I could run, but I walked as quickly as I could to the other side of the field and ducked into the bushes. The shade and the cover gave me a feeling of security; the thought that I may have been seen did not. The rest stop would have to wait.

I checked my compass heading and kept moving quickly through the sparse trees for another half an hour until I came upon a streambed. I quietly slid down the bank into it. It was not deep. This one was dry like so many others that I had found. I had to find water. "God, please help me find water," I said in a whisper. I decided to follow it for a while as it turned back and forth. It was running mainly south, and for some reason I thought that this one seemed more promising than the others.

I walked slowly, keeping a watch on the higher ground above the banks. This was not a deep ravine; it was only two or three feet deeper than the surrounding terrain. I was just about to give up when I stepped over a log and almost put my foot in the only water I had seen since this morning. This puddle, and it was hardly more than that, was similar to the water I had found the day before; it was stagnant and covered in dark slime and insects. I sat on my knees and used my hands to skim off the scum and make myself a clear area in the middle of the puddle. I tried to quietly scoop up the water. I drank as much as I could hold and cursed that I did not have a canteen.

It suddenly occurred to me that I did have my boots. What if I took off one of my boots and filled it with water? It probably would not hold more than an average tumbler. Was that worth it? Hell, yes! But it would not be watertight; the water would leak through the leather and also evaporate pretty quickly especially in this heat. Still, it would be some water that I could take with me. I took off my right boot and filled it with water. I would have to be careful. I did not want to run something sharp through my foot. I was already blind and burned, but I still had the use of both hands and both feet.

I stayed by the water for some time and drank as much as I could without vomiting. I continued to watch for anyone who might be following me since I crossed the clearing. I decided it was time to get going. I started walking, or hobbling, armed with my boot full of water. I had tied the laces tight and filled the boot with as much water as I could get in it. It did not take long to lose the water above the gap between the tongue and lace grommets. The actual foot part of the boot was the only thing really holding any water, and I carried that as if I had a boot full of diamonds.

I plodded along for what must have been hours with my boot in my left hand and my revolver in my right. I had lowered the hammer by now. I wanted to take a drink every few minutes, but I did not allow myself to do that; I had to save the precious water as long as I possibly could. I continued to follow trails when they were generally moving south-southeast and abandoned them when they were not. I had a set routine by now. I did not waste much time on a trail that was not taking me where I wanted to go. I had by now come to realize that if I did leave a trail behind, it was no big deal; I would find another within a short time.

Walking with one boot was really awkward and uncomfortable. I was just about to sit down and take a break, when I saw a burned out area ahead of me. I walked down the trail towards it and realized that, although the logs and trees were still smoldering, this fire had probably actually started yesterday or the day before. My guess was that my own people, Apache Scouts and Cobra gunships, had accidently started the fire with machineguns and rockets. I did not see any craters from Air Force bombs, and I was sure we did not have any artillery in the area that could reach this far north. I didn't know whether the ARVNs did or not.

I studied the surroundings as best I could with my "good" eye. I still had to tilt my head way to the left and to the rear to see, and it still hurt to do that. I was not sure just how large the burned-out area was. Some trees were burned, and others were spared. Most of the grass and bushes had burned.

I walked along the trail trying not to make footprints in the ashes. I thought it was probably not a good idea to stay in the vicinity long. This was not dense jungle; it was more like forest, and now that the scrub brush and bushes were burned away, the area was very open. Too open, I had lost my advantage of concealment. Apache Troop would not have shot up the place unless something or somebody had been there. Maybe they still were.

I hurried through the burned out region as quickly as I could and found myself back in undisturbed jungle. I had not seen or heard anyone, but that did not mean that they had not seen or heard me. By now my water was gone; I had decided it was better to drink it rather than watch what was left of it seep out of the porous leather and evaporate. I had taken several small drinks out of it. It had lasted a few hours and had turned out not to have been a bad idea. But it was nice to have both boots on again.

The sun was getting low. I needed to find water and a place to hide for the night. What day was this, anyway? I was shot down on the 10th; it must be March the 12th, or did I already lose track? I had spent the first night in the thicket of thorns, and the second night behind the two trees that formed the "V" overlooking the streambed. Yeah, this would be the third night: shit! Three days and three nights and still no rescue. Well…maybe tomorrow. I started walking; I needed water, and I had to find a place to hide.

I had been traveling south-southeast praying for water as I walked. I was hungry. I had encountered several streams, all dry. I dropped down into still another empty tributary that seemed to be generally going the right direction, and followed it. Fifty meters or so in front of me, I saw what I hoped was going to be water. But it did not look like water. From this distance whatever it was appeared to be black. In fact, it appeared to be a big fat black snake. I quickly stopped and considered the possibilities. I did not want to get into an argument with a damn python or a cobra or whatever. I knew there were a lot of venomous snakes in Southeast Asia. I thought that would be ironic, to get killed by a damn cobra!

It also occurred to me that it could be a crocodile. I had seen a lot of those in Vietnam, usually sunning themselves on a log or on the bank of a river. But that did not make any sense; they would be wherever the water was. Whatever it was was not moving, and as I cautiously closed the distance, it became obvious that it was flat and it was not a snake. It was water!

The water was lying in a five or six foot depression in the bottom of what was otherwise a bone-dry creek bed. Once again, I had prayed for water, and within a brief time I found it. It was filthy and stagnant and covered with water spiders, but it was water, and I was not complaining.

I had concentrated so much on not running into the enemy that the thought I might tangle with some large animal had never really occurred to me. Where were all the animals, anyway? I had not seen any animals, large or small. I was not complaining about that either.

I once again parted the scum and spiders as best I could and took a long-awaited drink. I now had water for the night. After drinking all the water I could and not vomiting, I began to look for a place to spend the night. I needed what I had found the night before, a concealed position that would give me some protection. I did not see anything like that. Unlike the streambed the night before, this stream was not in a deep ravine. The creek was only a few feet lower than the surrounding ground. I traveled down the ditch hoping to find something more suitable. After five or ten minutes, the ravine had become a little deeper, and I crawled up the bank to look around. I saw a knoll that was prominently higher than its surroundings. It was twenty meters or so away from the river bank. There were two trees on the stream side of the knoll and thick bamboo to its rear. This might work, I thought.

The two trees did not come together at the base as the two had the night before. I would need to fix that. But I could "plug" the hole with some bushes and try to camouflage it. I looked at the area behind the knoll. No trails, nothing, just thick bamboo. From that position behind the trees I would not be able to see down in the creek as I had the night before; maybe that didn't matter. The main thing was that I would be able to see, or at least hear, anyone approaching me from the river bank. I would not be able to see through the bamboo to my rear, but no one else would be able to see through it either, especially after it got dark, and that was happening fast.

I cut some bushes with my knife and placed them between the two trees trying to make them look as natural as possible. In a few minutes it would be dark, and it would not make any difference how natural they looked. After a few minutes, I was satisfied that no one would be able to see me behind my barrier. I decided that I had better get my last drink for the night. I did not need a stick to use as a marker since there was a log lying in the creek. That would be easy to find even in the quickly deteriorating light.

I hurried up the stream and got my last gulp of water for the night. I came back a few minutes later, found the log and then my hiding place; it was already getting difficult to see. This place was not as well hidden as my den of thorns had been, but I did not believe the bad guys would be able to see me or find me in this position unless they had seen me walking to it. I had tried to be quiet. I had also tried to be careful not to leave any tracks around the water or where I climbed out of the creek bed.

I was hungry, and I needed a cigarette. I wondered if they were dry yet. I reached in my leg pocket and took out the pack of Marlboros that I had not opened. They were still sealed, but they were also still wet. I thought maybe I could find a way to dry them overnight. I tore the cellophane wrapper off and then tore the Marlboro package down one side. I flattened out the piece of paper and laid it on the ground to dry. Then I took the mush that had been 20 cigarettes and ground it up in my hands. I laid that out on some leaves and hoped it would all be dry in the morning. I figured I would probably be able to "roll" one cigarette, maybe two, into the amount of paper I had from the wrapper.

I settled in for what was going to be my third night in the jungle.

I had not been sleeping long when I was awakened by a noise. Had I dreamed that, or had I really heard it? I heard it again. It was not a dream; there was something out there. I heard it again; something was moving slowly through the jungle. I lay silently in my hiding place. My uncocked .38 was on the ground next to me. I didn't move; I didn't breath. There it was again. The jungle was silent except for whatever, or whoever, was out there trying to walk quietly in dry leaves. I wondered if tigers hunted at night. It was different this time; there was more than one of them. There were at least three, and they were human.

I knew exactly what they were doing; I had done the same thing hunting with my dad. Walk a short distance, stop and listen, walk a short distance, stop and listen. They were looking for something or someone.

I stayed absolutely silent. I don't think I took a breath. I wanted my heart to stop beating and making so much noise. I don't know how close they passed by me. I lay there listening to them as they continued on their search, never knowing how close they actually were to me. I wondered if they were looking specifically for me. Maybe walking and listening like that was the way they always traveled at night. But why only three of them? That was not a platoon, not even a squad. That was more like one of our American five man LRRP (Long Range Reconnaissance Patrol) teams. But why would they be moving at night in such a small group? We were not supposed to have any Americans on the ground over here, not that that meant anything.

The intermittent walking and stopping continued for 30 to 40 minutes. After a while I could no longer hear them. I was mentally and physically exhausted, and I eventually fell back asleep.

Sometime in the middle of the night, I awoke to the sound of helicopters. At first I thought maybe I was dreaming, but I was not dreaming. There was no question that the sound was helicopters, and they sounded like Hueys. It sounded like there were at least three or maybe four of them. There was no mistaking that sound; those were rotor systems struggling with a load. It sounded as though they were putting in an air assault. But who would be putting that many troops in at night? We did not do that. We often inserted or extracted LRRPs at night, but those were five-man teams, and for that you only needed one Huey.

Ground operations in Cambodia were being conducted solely with the ARVN, and I was sure they would refuse to be inserted at night. Whoever they were, they were not there for me. My guys would not risk an insertion for me unless they knew exactly where I was, and even then they would not attempt it at night. If they knew where I was, they would make the rescue attempt at "first light" the next morning.

Well, somebody was out there. But who the hell were they? The NVA did not have any aircraft south of the DMZ, or at least, not that we knew of. Damn it, someone was flying helicopters, and they were only a few klicks away. I continued to listen for a few more minutes, and then they were gone. Once again, I fell asleep.

Chapter Fourteen

We arrived at Song Be late afternoon or early evening. It was still light. I was anxious to see what my new home was going to look like. It did not look like much. More red dirt and more red dust. It was obvious that the farther north I went, the farther away from Division "Rear," the more primitive the living conditions. Song Be, or Fire Support Base Buttons, as it was officially named, was much smaller than Phuoc Vinh, just as Phuoc Vinh was much smaller than Bien Hoa.

A lot of people were crowded around the mess tent, and I went ahead and got in line. Needless to say, I stuck out like a sore thumb in my new still-clean and still-green flight suit. The flight suits of the pilots and crews who had been here for a while had a red tinge, not really green anymore. I would later find out that that was because the hootch maids washed our clothes by hand, or actually by feet, in lake water brought over from the town.

People said "hello," and I introduced myself. Someone told me where to bunk. The main officers' quarters, more like a bunk house, was a covered central structure with a row of small drainage culverts jutting out along each side of the central building. Each culvert was very low; even I had to bend over to enter the one I had been given for the night. There was only enough room for a cot along one side of the curved corrugated steel wall and room on the floor (or under your cot) to put your gear. No room for anything else. The culvert was not much longer than the cot, and it barely fit in there.

Someone must have seen the look on my face as I surveyed the living conditions because he said, "Don't get too used to it; we're moving tomorrow."

I said, "What?" I was thinking, "I just got here."

"Yeah, we're moving across the old berm tomorrow. The engineers have been building us new living quarters and a new TOC (Tactical

Operations Center). They expanded the old berm on out to the north and west. So you lucked out, new guy. You won't have to live like this after tonight."

He was right; first thing in the morning we were told to move all of our stuff to the new hootches they had built for us. It was up to us to figure out how to move everything. Luckily, all I had was my baggage; I had not acquired anything yet like the guys who had been here for a while.

Early in the morning, I ran into WO1 Bob Spencer, one of my classmates at Ft. Rucker. He said he had already picked a place, and there was room for me. The plan was that each officer's hootch would house four guys; it did not matter if you were a warrant or a commissioned officer. There was one spot left if I wanted it. Sure, I wanted it.

"New Apache," as it was called, was going to be a lot nicer. Two rows of six corrugated galvanized steel hootches had been built at each end of our AO (living Area of Operation). These were longer, wider, and higher than the others in the old living area. They were roughly 18 feet long or so and maybe 12 feet wide. There were two rows of these at each end of our living area. One set for officers on the west end of the AO and another set for the enlisted men and the NCOs on the east end.

The hootches were placed side by side butted up against each other. Even though the side walls were curved in, I could stand in the middle of the room and not have to bend over. Of course, I was also shorter than everybody else.

The engineers had placed plywood on each end of the hootch with an opening for a door, but it was going to be up to us to build doors if we wanted them. Since the monsoons were starting, we were going to need doors.

They had laid rubber mats over the top of the structure to keep water from pouring through where the sheets of galvanized steel were bolted together, and then dumped dirt and sandbags on top of that to protect us from mortars. The dirt was also deep enough to give us insulation from the heat, and sometimes we even had a breeze.

The TOC had been built about halfway between the officers' hootches and the enlisted hootches. The TOC was laid out like a capital "H" with four culverts connected by a central hallway. One room was to be Flt Ops (flight operations), one was to be a briefing room with a large map of the AO (Area of Operations) for our missions on the flat wall, and the other two were for storage and whatever.

Latrines and showers were located farther away from the hootches out towards the new berm (greenline). Aircraft maintenance was performed under two large steel-framed tents. The mess hall consisted of two GP Medium tents, one for eating and one for food preparation. There were CONEX boxes and other tents scattered around for other uses such as the Motor Pool. Supply and the Arms Room were both in CONEX boxes.

I met my other two roommates as Bob and I moved into our new quarters. We were in the second building from the far end of the innermost row. 1st Lt. Max Evans and Cpt. Jeff Young were nice guys and were going to be great roommates. Max, Apache 38, was a Huey pilot with the Headhunters, and Jeff had recently taken over as the new Scout Platoon Leader, referred to as "White." Each of the four of us chose a corner; Bob and I were across from each other. Our families began to refer to us as the "SHEY" Boys, short for Spencer, Houser, Evans, and Young. We thought it sounded like a rock band. We would receive packages addressed to the SHEY Boys.

As the days and weeks went by, we acquired what we considered necessities: the engineers wired the hootches for electricity, and we bought a small Sanyo refrigerator from a guy who was leaving to go home. We shared the refrigerator, but we each bought our own fan and a radio or a cassette player. Bob's sister in California regularly sent him cassette tapes that she had recorded from a Los Angeles radio station that played the top hits of the week.

Max and I started working on doors. His put mine to shame. He built a split "Dutch" door for the end of the building that he shared with Cpt. Young. It had a piece of plastic in the top section for a window. It was really nice. Compared to their door, ours looked like shit. I had found some wood and some hinges from ammo boxes to make the door. I used a piece of an old inner tube in place of a spring to keep the door closed. But Max's door was really impressive. I guessed he did really well in shop class.

Our hootches had plywood floors about a foot above the ground. We lived above the floors, and the rats lived below. At night they came up to look for whatever food we may have left out: cookies, and crackers, whatever. In the rainy season they drowned under there. The plywood floors were butted up against the side walls, but because the walls were corrugated, there was an opening every few inches all the way down the side of each wall. The holes left plenty of room for the rats to come out anywhere they wanted all along both walls.

The one and only light bulb we had in the hootch hung in the middle of the room. The rats did not like the light, so they would wait until one of us had twisted the light bulb off for the night and had gotten comfortable before they would come out to search. You could hear their claws racing up and down the plywood like a dog on a hardwood floor. As soon as one of us got up to twist the bulb back on, they were under the floor again. This went on most nights. One night I dreamed, or I thought I dreamed, that a rat had run across my back in the middle of the night scratching me with its claws. The next morning Bob noticed scratches on my back. There was no other explanation as to how that might have happened; I didn't have a knife or anything sharp in my cot that could have done it. I never did figure it out, but the scratches were real.

From time to time we would hear someone in the other row of hootches fire a weapon blindly at the rats. Of course, they missed, and the rounds ricocheted off the rounded steel walls several times before coming to rest. I am still amazed that no one was hurt.

We played cards most nights, ate popcorn and peanut butter sandwiches, and drank either soda pop or beer. My dad sent us Jiffy Pop popcorn, and we filled a spent 105 mm shell casing with fuel and heated the aluminum container over that. That worked pretty well. We mainly played various games of poker. I tried to limit myself to losing no more than $10 a game. That usually worked unless someone wanted to play "Guts"; then it was easy to lose your ass.

I was assigned to the Scout Platoon under Cpt. Jeff Young, the new "White," but in the meantime while I was waiting for an in-country transition to the OH-6, I was filling in as an FNG (fucking new guy) co-pilot in the Lift Platoon. My first combat assault mission was flying with Apache 33, WO1 Ron Glass. All went well; the LZ for the insertion and the extraction were "cold." I learned a lot from 33 and the other experienced ACs, valuable knowledge that would help me no matter what I was flying, but I was anxious to get my OH-6 transition.

For a while I bounced back and forth between the Lift Platoon and the Scout Platoon, one day flying as observer in the left seat of a Scout bird and the next flying as "Peter Pilot" (co-pilot) in the Lift Platoon. I wanted to learn the Scout mission and how to handle the aircraft.

Eventually I was flying as observer/trainee every day, making my rounds from one Scout Pilot and his aircraft and crew to the next. I learned from all of them. I flew the aircraft, *if they let me,* usually at altitude on the way to a mission or on the way back. Scout missions were flown by only one pilot unless they were training someone. From time to time some Huey pilot wanted to ride along, but not very often.

I flew a lot with Apache 13, CW2 Joe Schlein, and Apache 15, WO1 Bill Frazer. Both were well experienced long-time Scout pilots. Joe was considered "old" by all of us; he was 30 or 31. Apache 11 and Apache 18, WO1 Bob Long and WO1 Stanley McCaw respectively, were also well experienced.

I learned that the OH-6 was an amazing aircraft. I still loved the ever-forgiving versatile Huey, but the OH-6 was different, like apples and oranges. It was very quick and agile. You barely moved the cyclic control to get any kind of response. It was almost like you just thought about the movement, and the aircraft responded. Very much like the TH-55 I had flown at Ft. Wolters also produced by Hughes.

Other cavalry units were beginning to use the OH-58 Jet Ranger. Like the Huey and the Huey Cobra, the OH-58 was built by Bell Helicopter. As much faith as I had in Bell, I did not see any way the OH-58 could replace the OH-6, not as a Scout bird. In some other capacity sure, but not as a Scout. Supposedly Bell had beaten out Hughes on the latest contract for an LOH. None of us could believe that. We took off every day with three of us on board, an M-60 machine gun, three M-16s, an M-79 grenade launcher, 2200 rounds of ammunition for the M-60, another ammo box full of grenades and homemade bombs, and a full load of fuel. Now how was an OH-58 going to do that?

The rumor was that Lady Bird Johnson had a lot of stock in Bell Helicopter and that President Johnson had pressured the Army to buy another Bell product. We did not know if there was any truth to any of that, but that was a commonly expressed rumor. And it certainly was true that Bell was based in Ft. Worth, Texas, Johnson's home state.

No one was saying that the 1st of the 9th was going over to the OH-58 and certainly none of us would go willingly. We learned to love the

OH-6, and everyone agreed that if you had to crash (and if you stayed in Scouts for very long, you were going to crash), that was the aircraft you wanted to be in. It was the most crashworthy aircraft in the inventory, and that was proven.

Through a long slow process I finally completed my OH-6 transition. By that time I had flown as observer on many missions and had flown with every Scout Pilot we had. I had learned the mission from the best. Along the way I was assigned the call sign "Apache 12." I was given the call sign long before I finished the transition. The problem was finding an IP (Instructor Pilot). We had to borrow one from another troop when they had one available. That meant that I had to either go to where that troop was, usually Echo Troop at Lai Khe, or the IP had to come to Song Be. A huge waste of time. As a result, I only received actual documented IP instruction once or twice a week.

One of my friends, Mike "Chaney" Powell, Apache 19, was sent to Vung Tau down on the coast southeast of Saigon to an actual school transition. I did not know why they did not send me there. Mike was back within a week or two having spent most of his time on the beach. Yes, I was jealous. In the meantime I flew almost every day continuing to learn the mission. And that was good.

Shortly after I officially finished the transition and was "signed off," I was told to take an aircraft and crew and go conduct a Scout mission. White showed me an area on the map over towards the town of Song Be. He gave me barriers to not cross, basically part of a grid square. The idea was that I should go over there as if I were on a real mission and "work" the area. There would be no Cobra coverage; it was an area where quote, "You shouldn't get into any trouble there."

I conducted the "mission" as if it was real, and it went well. I reported what I was looking at over the intercom since I had no Cobra to talk to. My tight right-hand turns became tighter as we burned off fuel, and I became more comfortable flying from the right seat. My hours of observing were all from the left seat. I had only flown in the right when I was with an IP. We found nothing, as planned, and had a good time. It was a great confidence builder.

Within the next couple of days I was assigned my own aircraft, #67-16273, and flew my own missions, real missions. Being given my own call sign and then being given my own aircraft were two of the proudest days of my life. I was recognized as Apache 12, and now I felt like I was truly fitting in. I was now a part of the brotherhood of Army combat helicopter pilots. I was 20 years old.

The weeks and the months went by, Bob flying in the Lift Platoon, me flying in Scouts. In the evenings we would share that day's experiences and close calls. Max shared most of that with us. Laughing about stupid mistakes we had both made. Days of the week meant nothing; most of us did not know what day of the week it was. There was no reason to know: there were no weekends, no Sundays, no holidays, and every day was the same. You were either flying that day or you were not, depending on mission assignments made by your platoon leader.

Every once in a while Bob and I would get a day off on the same day. There was really nowhere to go on FSB Buttons. From time to time we would walk over to the PX to buy Cokes or cigarettes or just to have something to do. It took about 15 minutes to walk over there. It was very small and there really was not much there, but we would go anyway. They usually had some American name brand of toothpaste and deodorant. I would buy greeting cards when they had them, but there was never much of a selection, so I bought whatever was available and changed the greeting to suit the occasion. I sent my mom a birthday card for Mother's day, a Christmas card for her birthday, just whatever I could find. It was the thought.

There was a really nice PX in Saigon, but we rarely had a chance to go there. I bought my first Seiko watch in the Bien Hoa PX. It seemed like everyone new to Vietnam bought a Seiko watch and a camera. A lot of guys bought stereos; some sent them home without ever opening the boxes.

Prices were amazingly low. The larger PXs had all the American-made name brands of cigarettes and alcohol. I smoked Marlboro "Reds," "cowboys." I was now up to three packs a day. You had to buy cigarettes by the carton, no single packs, but a carton was only $1.70; no sales tax, no state excise tax, no federal tax, 17 cents a pack!

I often had older NCO's ask me to pick up beer or a bottle of whiskey or some other alcohol for them if they knew I would be flying to Bien Hoa or someplace where I would have the opportunity. That was a switch, having me buy alcohol for someone older. Every time I had been home on leave I had tried to buy alcohol at the local carry out liquor stores in my hometown in Indiana where the drinking age was twenty-one. I could never get served even using my military ID or wearing my uniform. I could fight for my country (and possibly die for my country) but I could not legally buy a beer in Indiana. I also could not vote.

Part IV

13 March 1971

Day Four

Chapter Fifteen

I awoke from a sound sleep to the smell of smoke and rice cooking. I was not sure which direction the smell was coming from. There did not appear to be any wind. I had no way of knowing how far away the cook fire was. I did not believe it could be very far. The vegetation here was more like forest than jungle, and with any wind I supposed it could move through the trees easily. I lay quietly on my back in my hiding place, listening but not moving. I was looking at the rays of sunlight streaming down through the branches above me. I judged the time to be eight or nine o'clock again. "I must be in a routine now," I thought to myself, "or maybe the sun in the morning always looked like it was eight or nine o'clock."

There was no obvious change in my vision; my left eye remained useless, and my right was still blurry. I continued to have to cock my head to the extreme left and rear to be able to see out of the "bottom" of my right eye. Maybe I would never get my vision back.

There were no sounds, nothing, just silence. I quietly rolled to my side and tried to get a look towards the stream. I did not see anyone. I wished I could make out the direction the smell was coming from. It was a wood fire, and someone was cooking rice. But who? If they were ARVNs they were my ticket out of there. But it was much more likely that they were NVA, and how would I know until it was too late? If I got close enough to see their uniforms and equipment, they would undoubtedly see me first or hear me. Well, maybe not the ARVNs, but the NVA would for sure. The North Vietnamese had not made it all the way down the Ho Chi Minh Trail from North Vietnam by being careless and stupid.

There was another possibility; I wondered if they were Cambodian farmers. Probably not; most of them had left the area because of the fighting. And I knew they were not Cambodian soldiers; they would have made sure they were nowhere near the North Vietnamese troops. Our army shared intelligence with the Cambodian government, and we knew that once we told them where the NVA were, their armies literally went the other direction. That was the smart thing for them to do; they were no match for North Vietnamese "regulars." Of course, neither were the ARVNs.

I thought about my options. I could not just start walking around looking for the people with the campfire. If I walked up on them and they were "bad guys," I would be dead. If they were the "good guys," I still might be dead. If I *was* able to determine that they were ARVNs, how would I approach them without being shot? I would expect them to shoot at the first sign of movement.

I had my pen-flares, but I could not use those unless I was absolutely convinced they were *South* Vietnamese. I still had to be able to see them to be sure. Meanwhile, I had to stay still and be quiet.

While I thought about it, I noticed the tobacco I had laid out the night before to dry. I picked some of it up and worked it around in my fingers. It had not dried; it was still mush. I thought it would have dried by now. I sprinkled the tobacco into the leaves around me so that it could not be seen. I took the Marlboro wrapper I had laid out, rolled it up in a tiny ball, and buried it under some leaves. The ultimate "field strip." Damn, I really would have liked to have had a cigarette. Maybe it was just as well; the smell of a cigarette would travel through the woods just as easily as the smell of rice. And American cigarettes had a different smell than Vietnamese cigarettes. Vietnamese cigarettes smelled like they were made from manure. Maybe they were.

I waited about an hour until the smell of the rice cooking had dissipated. I knew that did not necessarily mean the people were gone; they could still be nearby. I wanted to get moving, and I was thirsty. I had been silently listening and not moving for what I thought was now more than an hour. I decided to stand up. Nothing was moving or making a sound to my rear in the thick bamboo. I cautiously rose up and peered over the fence of bushes I had built.

I could not see anyone; I did not detect any movement, nothing. No wind, no sound, no smell, nothing. I took a few steps out of my hiding place and surveyed the surrounding area; still nothing. I cautiously headed down the stream to my watering hole to get one last drink before I headed out for the day.

I found my pool of water and looked around on the ground for any footprints or any other indication that someone had been there. I found nothing. I knew the enemy would be carrying water, but they might be smart enough to know I was not and that I would need to find it. They might be checking these pools as they came across them.

I drank as much water as I could hold and headed back down the creek. I climbed up the bank, careful not to leave marks, and looked around my hiding place one last time. Between the crash and the sleeping conditions, I was very stiff and sore, even worse than I was the morning before. I took one last look and then started walking south-southeast.

I decided that I was going to find something today. I was going to make it to Snuol or somewhere, but I was going to find *something* today. Unless I had miscounted and lost a day, this should be March the 13th. I could not keep going with no food. I wasn't really hungry; the stomach contraction pains were gone now, but I knew I could not keep going much longer without any nourishment. I had to either make it to Snuol or be picked up by one of our aircraft. But it had to be *today*.

As I walked, I realized that my confidence had continued to grow. I was not now overconfident or careless, but mentally I had come a long way since the day I was shot down. In the first few minutes of the first day, I had believed that I would either be captured or killed within minutes, if not seconds, of crawling out of the river. When that did not happen, I knew I would be captured or killed within the first hour. After

I made it through the first day, I was sure that I would be caught by the NVA the second day. None of that happened. I was by no means safe now, but as I put more time and distance between myself and the crash site, my confidence grew. I still walked with my revolver in my hand, but I had stopped carrying it cocked. I did not want an accidental discharge.

I knew that I would not be safe until I was picked up by Americans, but it made sense to me that the farther south I traveled and the closer I got to Snuol, the less likely I would encounter NVA troops. I knew from flying past Snuol every day that the dense jungle in the area where I was shot down would thin out into forest; I was already seeing that. And the forest would have more and more clearings and open areas in the vicinity of Snuol. The North Vietnamese would not want to be caught out in those open areas.

There was a rubber plantation surrounding Snuol that gave them cover and concealment. They had been hiding there at the beginning of the campaign, but they had moved north as American aircraft came into the area to support the ARVN division headquartered at Snuol. We did not believe they were hiding there now. A large group of NVA troops would be discovered that close to Snuol even in the rubber. Still, that did not mean there were no North Vietnamese between me and the Snuol compound. They could still have patrols just outside of Snuol.

I had been walking now for four days. I had not traveled far that first day. I believed that my direction of movement was almost all westerly that day. But the second and third days I stayed on what I thought was a good south-southeast course. I *had* to be closer to Snuol and the ARVN compound there. But, how close, I had no idea how far I had come. If I could just make it to that compound, they would have food and water and just as important…radios. "I had to make it there today," I said to myself.

As I traveled, there were more and more open areas, a good indication that I really was getting closer to Snuol. I knew it would be much safer to stay in the tree line and go around them, but now the problem was the exact opposite of what I had encountered in the thick jungle: now there were *too many* open areas. There was no way for me to avoid or go around all the clearings that I was now finding. I had to pass through them and hope that I would not be seen.

As I walked along a trail, I saw ahead of me that there was another clearing coming into view. This one was different; there was hootch in it. I stopped where I was and listened carefully. I did not smell a cook fire, and I did not see or hear anyone. I continued to move cautiously up to the tree line and knelt there behind a tree. There was more than one hootch; there were three that I could see. The clearing had been a rice paddy at one time, and the hootches appeared to be very old. I looked around the clearing as best I could and, seeing nothing, decided to walk up to the closest hootch. I looked inside, hoping to find something that might be useful to me, maybe something to carry water in. There was nothing.

I was correct: the hootch was old and appeared to have been abandoned a very long time. The other two hootches were scattered 40 or 50 yards away and appeared to be in the same condition. I decided it probably was not a good idea to stay out in the open any longer than I had to, so I did not investigate the other two. It seemed very unlikely that anything I might find of value to me would have been left behind. These huts had probably been looked at by both armies many times.

I had been walking for what I thought was probably half an hour since leaving the three hootches when I saw an unusual tree to my right, ten or twelve feet off the trail. It had some kind of greenish brown fruit growing on it. The fruit, or whatever it was, was eight to ten inches long, fat and elongated. The objects were similar in shape to bananas but fatter and longer, and were hanging individually, not in clusters. I did not recognize the tree or the fruit and had never seen anything like it. I did not know what it was, so I certainly did not know if it was edible. I smelled it, and although I was hungry and really tempted, I did not taste it.

How long had it been since I had eaten? I was shot down on March the 10th, and I thought it was now the 13th. I did not eat on the 10th; my last meal must have been some time on the 9th. Four days, four days since I had eaten. I was hungry, but I was not yet to the point of eating something I did not recognize and might be poison. I wondered how long it would take me before I would be willing to eat *anything*. I considered taking some of the fruit with me, but I decided not to, and left the tree as I had found it. I hoped I had not passed up on some kind of perfectly safe delicious damn breadfruit or something like it.

I was very hot, and I needed water. I prayed that I would find it soon. I walked for what I thought was another hour, maybe two, in and out of forests and clearings. As I came to the edge of one of these relatively large clearings, I found what looked to be a trash pile of clear plastic bags. They had been tossed on what had been some type of a fire, probably a fire for cooking. As I inspected the plastic bags, I realized they had at one time contained rice, and a few still had some kernels in them.

This was how the South Vietnamese troops carried their rice. The North Vietnamese carried theirs in tubes. Of course, this could have been ARVN rice captured and eaten by the NVA, but I did not believe they would just leave the bags here to be found, unless they wanted them to be found. I thought about collecting a few bags to hold water, but they all seemed to be torn too badly. I left them and moved on.

I was getting tired and as always very thirsty. I continued to move from wooded areas to clearings. Some of the openings or clearings in the trees were small, and some were so large that I thought they had probably once been rice paddies. This was not what I considered jungle anymore; this was more like an Indiana woods. This went on for quite some time until finally I walked out of the trees and came to the edge of still another clearing. I saw a cluster of lush green bamboo surrounded by tall green grass. It looked out of place. It *was* out of place. Nothing was that shade of green in the dry season. I had not really noticed any bamboo since the previous day. But there it was, green, not yellow-brown like all the other grasses. As I got closer, I saw why.

As I approached, there seemed to be a natural archway opening in the bamboo inviting me to enter. As I bent down and ducked to get under the overhanging bamboo branches, I was transformed to another world. There in front of me was a beautiful crystal clear pool of water, more like a small pond. This was *fresh* water, not a stagnant pool; this was a spring, a natural spring! It was an oasis in the middle of an otherwise desert dry jungle! I could not believe it! I turned around and looked back outside to see if anyone was watching or following. I did not see or hear anyone or anything. I looked back at what I had found; I could not believe my eyes. "Thank you, God," I said to myself out loud, hoping no one heard. I drank as much as I could hold, and then I drank again.

I wanted to stay there awhile and rest. What I really wanted was to lie down in the shade of the bamboo in that beautiful spot and take a nap. The growth of bamboo was such that once inside it was difficult to see out and practically impossible for someone to see in. But that did not make it safe; the whole growth of bamboo looked so foreign to the area that you may as well have put a big neon sign "look over here" on it. Or a Day-Glo orange target.

I also realized that any treasure like this had to be well known in the local area. The North Vietnamese would have to have the spring marked on their maps. They would be coming here to use this, and probably often. But as I looked around, there was no sign whatsoever of any type of activity, no footprints human or animal. The bushes and the grass were not smashed down or pushed aside by anxious individuals or animals trying to get to the water. The area was completely undisturbed. That didn't make any sense.

I walked to the other end of the pool, and there was another archway of bamboo similar to the one I had entered. I walked "outside" and surveyed the area, and there was nothing. I had the oasis to myself, at least for the moment. Once again I had prayed for water and in a short time I found it. Like manna from Heaven. I did not want to leave.

I stayed for a while, drank as much water as I could hold without vomiting, and left my "Garden of Eden." I needed to find something to carry water in.

I continued to move south-southeast following trails in and out of trees and clearings and then was suddenly startled by something running through the brush. It was not a man; it was a small animal, but it still scared the shit out of me. Then it came out of the bushes and ran across the trail, and I realized it was a chicken! "What the hell was a damn chicken doing out here?" I wondered. That had to mean that there was a village around here somewhere, didn't it? A village meant food and people, but which people?

They would be Cambodian villagers, not Vietnamese, but would they be friendly and help me? The fighting inside their country by the North Vietnamese, the South Vietnamese, and the Americans had caused a lot of turmoil and destruction, and no doubt, Cambodian lives. It would be hard to blame them for not being friendly.

The chicken kept running and escaped into the foliage. I had never had a clear shot, and even if I had, it would have been foolish to shoot. I would have missed, and in the meantime I would have let everyone in the surrounding area know that I was there. That was the first and only living thing I had actually seen, not counting water spiders and insects, since I had been shot down. Maybe that was a good thing.

The sun was high. "It must be mid day," I told myself. I came out of the woods into a large open area. Twenty or 30 yards in front of me was a pile of burned debris, resembling another trash pile but much larger. Nothing stood higher than my waist. As I got closer, I could see that it had been a structure, a house or a hootch. Whatever had started the fire had not left the occupants much time to take their belongings with them. I doubted they were even there when it happened; most Cambodians had left the area.

On the extreme left side of the house was a burned motorcycle that had obviously been inside. Maybe the owners had some little garage type of thing on the side of the house. Or maybe they actually had the motorcycle in the house. But like the rest of the hootch, the motorcycle was just a charred piece of junk now.

As I looked at the remains of the building and the motorcycle, I noticed a wide trail up to the building. It was more than a path or a trail; it was a hard-packed lane. As I followed it with my eye, it curved away from the hootch and crossed a ditch. But what now had my attention, and almost took the wind right out of me, was that on the other side of the ditch, the lane met a road! A road, a real road, not a trail or a road created by two tire paths, a *real* road! I almost ran to it.

It was not just a road; it was a hard surface road, not concrete or asphalt like back in the States, but what had been a tarred "hard stand" road. That was the best they had in Cambodia and in Vietnam. It was running generally north and south. I looked as far as I could see in both directions. "My God, It's Highway 13," I said to myself out loud. It had to be. Highway 13 was the only road out there like that, and it was running the right direction. It had to be Highway 13! It had to be. I had been looking for that road since the afternoon of the first day. "I'll be a son of a bitch," I thought.

There was no traffic on the road, not a bicycle, not a Lambretta, nothing. I kept the ditch between myself and the road, and started walking south paralleling the road. I thought I would be less obvious if I used whatever cover was available. But there was not much there. I stayed inside the tree line, if there was one. Sometimes there would be rubber trees for a while, sometimes other stands of trees or bushes, but about half the time it was completely open with nothing to hide me.

I traveled that way for a while ducking into bushes and cover when I could and proceeding out into the open when I had to. From time to time Highway 13 would have a side road come in to meet it in a "T" intersection. I always looked both ways up and down the side roads so that I would not be taken by surprise. About the third one of those roads I came to, I saw an old man and a boy standing with their bicycles in the middle of the road. There was no cover, and they had already seen me. Thankfully, they were not soldiers, and they were not armed.

They made no attempt to move towards me or to get away; they just stood there next to their bicycles smiling with sheepish grins. I was sure they were afraid but trying not to show it. I had not seen another human being for four days.

I approached them with my .38 in my right hand, and with my left hand grasped the handlebars of the older man's bike. He continued to smile at me with his betel nut black teeth. It was hard to tell how old either one of them was. I would have guessed the older man in his forties, maybe fifties, and the boy maybe in his teens.

I tugged the bicycle towards me and said, " I take, I take." I did not speak any Cambodian, and I was sure they did not speak any English. Maybe French, but that would not help me. I had taken Spanish in high school.

I pulled on the handlebars more firmly this time and said, "I take, I take," as I pointed my revolver at his head and cocked it. The old man released his grip, and I pulled the bicycle to me. He still had that stupid grin on his face. I hopped on the bike and started pedaling south towards Snuol. I hated taking his bike, but at that moment I needed it more than he did. I rode for a few minutes at an easy pace. My gun was still in my right hand, and it was difficult to hold on to the handgrip. I put my revolver back in my shoulder holster, so I could hold on with both hands.

After a few minutes I saw a red and white tombstone-shaped marker on the right side of the road. The first time I had seen those it was many months earlier in Vietnam, and I thought they *were* tombstones. As I got closer, I was able to read "Snuol" at the top of the marker and a "2" at the bottom. Was that possible? Could I really be only two miles from Snuol? Wait, those wouldn't be miles; those would be kilometers. That was even better. Was it possible that I was only two kilometers from Snuol? How could that be?

Still, I had been out there for four days, moving south-southeast most of the time. I had hoped to find Highway 13 either late that first day or the morning of the second day. That first day I now believed I had traveled mainly west, but beginning the second day I had tried to keep a good course south-southeast. So from a position somewhere probably southwest of the crash I started my south-southeast course. That would account for me being farther south than I thought I was, and for it taking me longer to find Highway 13. But could I really be only two kilometers from Snuol? I started pedaling faster.

The rubber trees were now on both sides of me. I had not seen another soul since the old man and the boy. Where was everybody?

I had not been on the bicycle very long when I heard a vehicle coming up the road from the south. I rode the bike off into the ditch, hid in the bushes, and drew my Smith & Wesson. I watched through the bushes as an American Jeep painted with ARVN markings drove by me. The canvas top was down, and I could clearly see two men in the Jeep dressed in ARVN uniforms. But I did not know if they really were ARVN; I was not going to trust anyone out there, but I wanted that Jeep. The vehicle went on up Highway 13 a hundred yards or so, pulled into a side road, and apparently dropped off the passenger. Then it turned around and started back towards me again. The driver was alone. I knew this would be my only chance to take the Jeep.

I moved through the bushes to the point where there was a small knoll above a curve in the road. As the Jeep drove by and slowed for the curve, I jumped from the knoll into the back of the Jeep, quickly crawled between the front seats, and pushed the barrel of the .38 into the driver's right ear. His eyes were as big as golf balls, and his mouth dropped wide open. I thought he might jump out of the Jeep.

"You take me Snuol!" I yelled, "You take me Snuol!" I cocked the gun.

"Yeah, I take, I take!" he yelled.

"You take me Snuol,…now!"

I looked around the Jeep; there were no weapons in the vehicle, and the man was not armed! "Unfucking believable," I thought. He *had* to be ARVN. Where the hell was I that this guy was nonchalantly driving around with no weapon? I would not even walk around in Saigon with no weapon. Fucking ARVNs!

I had no way of knowing if he really was ARVN and no way of knowing if he really was taking me to Snuol. We continued to drive south on 13, so I knew we were headed the right direction, and I was not walking or pedaling a bicycle. After a few minutes we turned west on a dirt side road. I was no longer sure about what we were doing. I pushed the barrel further into his ear.

"You take me Snuol!" I shouted.

"Yeah, I take, I take!" he said.

I still was not sure about my driver; I could have easily taken the Jeep, but I was not sure how to get from the highway to the compound. I had flown past the South Vietnamese compound every day for two-and-a-half weeks as we flew up the road from Loc Ninh. I knew that it was not actually on Highway 13, but sat to the west of it. I had, of course, never driven to it, and I could not remember how far west of the highway it was. I thought if this turned out to be a trick, I would shoot him, take the Jeep, and go back to the highway until I either found Snuol or ran out of gas.

After a few more minutes of driving on the side road, a bunker complex began to come into view; it was buried half underground. That could not be the NVA, not out in the open like that this far south; it had to be South Vietnamese. I began to believe that my driver really was ARVN, but that did not stop me from leaving my gun in his ear. We drove through a mine field and then through several different rows of concertina barbed wire. He obviously knew where he was going; I just hoped he was taking me to the right place. If this was the Snuol compound, I would have never known to turn on the dirt road that led to it, and I would have never seen it from Highway 13. I would have gone right on past it on that bicycle and eventually ridden across the border into Vietnam, if I wasn't shot or captured first.

He sped around several bunkers and then pulled up in front of the largest one and the one that looked the most official. Although there were no flags or markings of any kind, this one had about a dozen antennas surrounding it, and the generators were louder here than anywhere else. All of the bunkers were built mainly underground with only their tops showing. Mounds of dirt were piled on their roofs along with hundreds, if not thousands, of sandbags piled on the sides, all of which were to try to stop incoming mortars.

I saw that there was a set of steps going down into the bunker. I got out of the Jeep and still pointing my revolver at the man, I asked, "Snuol?" I repeated, "Snuol?"

"Yeah, yeah, Snuol!"

As I started toward the entrance, the ARVN soldier became agitated, and started yelling something at me in Vietnamese, which, of course, I did not understand. I finally figured out that he was trying to tell me that I could not take my gun into the bunker. I knew that there had been a rash of mutinies in the South Vietnamese Army, and some had included assassinations. Apparently soldiers were not allowed in the bunker with a weapon.

I put my gun in my left hand and with my right grabbed the right side of my collar where my warrant officer rank was sewn on, and thrust it out towards him.

"Officer, officer!" I shouted.

"Ah, yeah, yeah," he said, as he smiled with a look of some kind of recognition. I moved the gun back to my right hand and started down the steps into the bunker.

At the bottom of six or eight wooden plank steps, I literally ran into what I thought was a colonel. He looked shocked. I had forgotten that my face was completely burned and by now was covered with scabs. I could not imagine what I must have looked like, and for that matter, I didn't want to know.

"I need your radios," I said. "You speak English?"

"Yes, I speak English; who are you?" He spoke better English than I did.

"I'm an American," I stated the obvious. "I was shot down three days ago. I need to use your radios."

"Yes, we look for you. My men look all over for you."

"Well, you didn't look very damn well!" I shot back at the colonel. "I need your radios, Col. Truong." I had finally been able to read the embroidered name tape on his fatigues.

"Yes, we look all over for you."

It was obvious that I was in the right bunker; this was their TOC, the Headquarters of their division. The colonel led me to their communications center. It was a large room with radios and operators arranged all along one of the walls. They must have had ten or twelve FM radios, all, I assumed on different frequencies. Besides the radio operators, there were others working at various tables throughout the room. Maps and diagrams covered most of the walls.

I looked at the radios and back at the colonel. He motioned to me and told me to go ahead and use whatever I needed. I scooted one of the operators out of the way and dialed in the frequency that Apache Troop had been using the day I went down.

I "keyed" the mike button.

"Any Apache aircraft, any Apache station, this is Apache One-Two! Any Apache aircraft, any Apache station, this is Apache one-two!.........There was no answer just static and dead air. "Any Apache aircraft, any Apache aircraft, any Apache station, this is Apache One-Two!"......There was nothing; I could not believe it.

Col. Truong came over to me and seeing my frustration said, "It's all right, we know right frequency, we take care of it. We get you something to eat."

I was not thinking straight. I should have known that my people would have changed frequencies after losing an aircraft; that was just SOP (Standard Operating Procedure). You had to assume when you lost an aircraft that the enemy were able to get to it and look at the radios. It was also SOP for a downed pilot to change his frequencies and destroy his radios and the aircraft, time and situation permitting, just for that reason.

The colonel was being tactful; he knew all that, and he also knew that one of those radios in that room was already "up" and monitoring whatever the current Apache Troop frequency was. Hell, it might have been the radio I changed.

We walked out of the commo room and down the hall to another large room which turned out to be the officers' mess. There was a long table, and seated around it were more South Vietnamese officers than I had ever seen. I assumed that the big guy at the head of the table was a general; he had more shit on his uniform than the other guys, and I saluted. I tried to tell him who I was and why I was there, and he just looked first at me and then back to the colonel. It was obvious he did not speak English. The colonel explained in Vietnamese what was going on, and the general just nodded his head.

Col. Truong took me back down the hallway and sat me down at a small table against the wall. He said something to a couple of men and soon one of them returned with a C-ration can of sliced peaches. I sat down to my first meal in four days. Before I was able to start on the peaches, the other man appeared and handed me a tall clear glass and a Ba Muoi Ba (33) beer. It was cold. I tasted the peaches; they were also cold and delicious. I sat there a few minutes enjoying the peaches and the beer and the thought that it all might really be over soon. Truong had walked away for a few minutes and then came back.

"Colonel, were you able to get my people on the radio?" I asked.

"Yes, they come for you."

"When?" I asked.

"Soon, they come for you soon."

I was still eating peaches out of the C-ration can when I heard the unmistakable whop whop whop of a lone Huey. I started to stand up and fell back into the chair. My legs had quit working; they were rubber. The colonel had two soldiers pick me up, one under each arm, and carry me out of the bunker. I had my peaches in one hand and my glass of beer in the other. They walked me out of the bunker entrance and around the building. I could hear the Huey, but there was a large tree at the corner of the bunker blocking my view, so I was not yet able to see the helipad. We came around the tree, and there was the most beautiful sight in the world, an Apache Troop Huey at full operating RPM waiting on the helipad. I knew the pilots would not want to be on the ground long; the compound often got mortared when a helicopter landed.

The crew stared out at me in amazement. At first all they saw was a green uniform half walking, half being carried towards their aircraft. As we got closer to the helipad, they began to be able to make out an American flight suit. I could not recognize the crew yet; at this distance they all looked the same in helmets and flight suits. Besides the two door gunners there were other people in the back. They still had not recognized me. As we got still closer, they were able to see the "A" Troop 1st/9th patch on my chest pocket. I believe they were beginning to figure out *what* I was, but recognition of *who* I was seemed to hit all of the crew at the same time. The two pilot doors flew open, both pilots apparently wanting to get out at the same time.

I recognized Cpt. Tom Agness (Apache 36) sitting on my side of the aircraft in the right front seat. Meantime, Cpt. Jim Kurtz (Red) leaped out of his "jump set" in the back with his helmet still on never bothering to unplug and was running towards me. He grabbed me and gave me a big hug, and the two ARVNs who had helped me released me into Jim's arms. He basically threw me into the aircraft and strapped me in a jump seat. I looked up, and newly promoted Cpt. Max Evans (Apache 38), one of my old hootch mates back at Song Be, was in the front left seat. Max was the AC. He was all smiles twisting around in his seat so he could shake hands.

One of the two pilots decided they had what they had come for, and it was time to leave. The Huey nosed over, and we were south bound skimming over the rubber trees and climbing up through the hot dry air leaving Snuol behind. I did not have a helmet or headset, and everyone was trying to yell at me above the sound of the turbine engine. Besides Jim Kurtz and the two door gunners, there were two other men in the back sitting in crew seats against the transmission bulkhead. One was Vietnamese, and the other appeared to be Cambodian.

Jim, Max, and Tom were all smiling and laughing as they spoke into their "mic" booms on their helmets. I was not sure when they were talking to each other and when they were talking to someone outside the aircraft. I could not hear anything they said, but Tom turned around in his seat and yelled, "I just let the folks at Loc Ninh know we had you on board!"

"I can't hear you!" I yelled.

"I just told the guys at Loc Ninh that we had you on board! They don't believe me!"

"Are we headed there now?" I yelled.

Tom held up one finger motioning me to wait a minute. I could tell he was listening on the radio. Then he turned back to me.

"We're taking you direct to Phuoc Vinh to the hospital!" Tom yelled. "And it sounds like you're gonna have an escort!"

I knew we would be flying past Loc Ninh on the way to Phuoc Vinh, and I thought maybe we would be low enough that I would be able to see people walk out onto the runway and wave at us. But I did not expect what happened next. When word spread that "Apache 12" was alive and on the way back to Phuoc Vinh, people went crazy with disbelief and excitement.

Before we even reached Loc Ninh, we were joined by three Cobras, two on our right side and one on our left. Apparently the crews had unanimously decided to launch and see for themselves if it was true. They planned to escort us at least part of the way to Phuoc Vinh. They flew up close to us and waved. I waved back and toasted them with my beer. I moved back and forth from the right jump seat to the left to wave and make sure I saw everyone. Before I knew it, I was being treated to Cobras performing "hammerheads" and "wingovers". Jim made sure to tell me that good wishes were coming in over the radio from everywhere.

I continued to eat my peaches and wave.

Chapter Sixteen

The flight from Snuol to Phuoc Vinh went by very quickly, and in no time I began to be able to make out the corrugated steel roofs of the fire support base. We landed at Pinetree, and I was taken to the 1st of the 9th Aid Station, more like a clinic than a hospital, and examined by Dr. Kaplan. He immediately put an IV in my arm and dressed my burns. There was not a lot he could do with them; they were already healing or at least scabbed over. He determined that I was exhausted, dehydrated, and suffering from first and second degree burns. He also looked at my eyes and said he would make arrangements for me to see an optometrist in Saigon.

While he was examining me, a parade of Apache Troop personnel came in to see me, including Ace Miller, who could not have been any nicer to me. He told me not to worry about anything for a week and then we would talk about me flying again. The chaplain also came in to see me and tell me that they were going to put through a "Class A" (capable of calling outside Vietnam) phone call for me. Meanwhile all of the windows of the aid station were crowded with the faces of members of Apache Troop who were trying to get a look at me and wave to me.

The doctor wanted to keep me there at least 24 hours for observation, but I wanted to go back to my hootch in the Apache living area and be with people. I also knew there would be some kind of celebration, and I did not want to miss a thing. Dr. Kaplan gave in and decided it might do me more good to be back with my friends. He let me go back to my unit with the promise that I would not "over" exert myself, and that I would drink plenty of water. Water, not alcohol.

The chaplain made good on his promise to get a phone call through for me to the States, and I called my mother. I had asked before I talked to her if she had been told I was missing, and I was assured that she had not. I had called her once several months earlier from the USO in Saigon. It was obvious when I reached her that she did not know anything about what had happened, so I did not tell her. We had a "normal" conversation in which she asked how I happened to be able to call, and I just told her that I had the opportunity to use a Class-A phone. She accepted that, and we went on with our conversation. Little did I know that later that day two Army officers in a staff car from Ft. Benjamin Harrison in Indianapolis would come to see her and personally notify her that I had been Missing in Action.

The two officers, one a chaplain, tried to explain to her that I had been shot down and had been MIA for more than 72 hours. She, of course, told them that that was not possible, citing our earlier phone call and telling them "you have the wrong person." They eventually convinced her that they had the correct WO1 Craig J. Houser, but were not able to explain why I had not told her myself about the crash and the rescue.

My father was living just across the Ohio border in New Paris, and two Air Force officers from Wright-Patterson Air Force Base at Dayton finally tracked him down and found him fishing at a local stone quarry.

In both cases the personal visit was later followed up by a telegram that same day from the Department of the Army giving them the same information. Thankfully, the personal visits came before the telegrams.

I was released by the doctor, and I did go back to my hootch to rest. Ace Miller had told me I had a week off and to take it easy, and that was exactly what I intended to do. Bob Spencer was still in the hospital with malaria, which meant I had the hootch entirely to myself, but I did not count on the constant visits of well-wishers.

There was excitement and celebration in Apache; I was alive. As someone said, I had "come back from the dead," but the exhilaration was diminished for all of us because Robert Kiser was dead and Curtis Smoot was still missing.

I had asked about Kiser and Smoot as soon as I had the opportunity. I was told that Kiser's body had been recovered from the wreckage on the bottom of the river still strapped in his seat. SSG Nelson, one of our maintenance sergeants, had volunteered to go on the ground with the "Browns" when they were inserted. He went into the river and dove down to look for our bodies in the aircraft. There were numerous fragmentation wounds on Robert's body, but at that time it was unclear whether he had died of those wounds or drowned.

Smoot was still missing. Both of our flight helmets had been found floating downriver hung up in tree branches near the water's edge. American boot prints had also been found on the river bank at two different locations. Next to one set of boot prints were my missing flight gloves and very close by a brand new NVA pith helmet. The ARVN's had seen a lot of NVA boot prints all over the area. All of those things had been found very late in the afternoon of the first day after the North Vietnamese had pulled back north from the area following the Cobra attacks and three air strikes. Other than those things, there was no sign of what had happened to either of us.

It appeared that, like me, Smoot had somehow survived the crash, gotten out of the aircraft, and made it to the river bank. The search for Curtis continued for several more days. The feeling and the hope was that if I had lasted that long out there, maybe he had, too. But he was never found. Nothing about the crash was released to *Stars and Stripes* or to the general press until the search for Curtis was given up.

The following day I was sleeping in my hootch when a runner came to tell me that I was going to be picked up soon and taken to Division Headquarters. I was going to be Major General George Putnam's (the First Air Cavalry Division Commander) guest for dinner. They were sending a Jeep for me. I thought, "No way!" I did not have time to shower, and I could not shave because of the burns to my face; my beard was trying to grow through the scabs. It was not very pleasant to look at. I barely had time to put on my flight suit and boots. The Jeep came and took me to division. I was introduced to MG Putnam and sat next to him for his daily briefing.

I was told that as soon as the briefing was over, the general and I would have drinks at the club, and then have dinner at the general's mess. He was very gracious, and it was obvious that he was proud of me and all of Apache Troop.

I did not tell him that I had actually met him many months earlier when I had first arrived in Apache back at Song Be. I was smoking on the flight line next to a LOH when a Jeep drove by and made a "U" turn. It was MG Putnam stopping to make an "on the spot correction". He was nice even then. He just explained to me that he was sure I knew not to smoke within 50 feet of the aircraft, and that he could not have "his" young warrant officers setting a bad example. I had never spoken to a general before, much less a two-star general. I apologized and told him it would not happen again. He had been satisfied with that, and he and his driver went on their way. That seemed like so long ago.

I sat next to the general while "full" colonels and "light" colonels pointed to maps and gave a very lengthy briefing on what happened in the division AO today and what to expect tomorrow and in the future. An Air Force major wound up the briefing with a weather forecast for the next several days. He used all the meteorological terms for what was happening, but the "bottom line" summary was that it was going to be hot and dry. I thought to myself, "No shit! Hell, I could have told the general that."

After the briefing, we had drinks, and MG Putnam asked me a lot of questions about the Cambodian campaign and what we had seen "out there." I told him that I, of course, only had a limited knowledge of the "big picture," but the enemy that *I* had seen in Cambodia was well-disciplined, well-equipped, and very willing to fight. He just sort of nodded his head. He seemed to be digesting what I had said.

At one point MG Putnam asked me if we needed anything. I told him there was a shortage of nomex gloves and flight suits and all-leather boots. He seemed surprised. We had several of the newer guys, at least in Apache Troop, who had come to us from infantry units and were now flying as door gunners and observers in jungle fatigues, jungle boots, and without gloves. It was obvious he was not aware of that, and he told me so.

He knew full well that by regulation all flight crew members were required to wear nomex flight suits, nomex gloves, and all leather boots. Unlike cotton, nomex charred before it burned, and that gave you a few extra seconds in a fire. It was not fire proof, but it was much better than cotton. All-leather boots do not melt into your ankles like the "uppers" on nylon jungle boots. It had been his understanding that we were "in good shape" as far as flight gear was concerned. He called over some full colonel who was standing a few feet away at the bar talking to a couple of other officers.

"David, come here a minute."

"Yes, general," said the colonel, as he quickly walked over to us.

"Mr. Houser says that there is a shortage of nomex gloves and flight suits and all-leather boots in the 1st of the 9th. Is that true?"

The colonel turned to me and glared with that "If looks could kill" look. I am sure he thought, "How dare this young warrant officer make me look bad in front of the general?"

"I will look into it right away, general," the colonel said, and he walked away as if he was going to take care of it at that very moment. Or, he was going to wait for me outside.

I did not know what the colonel's job was, but it appeared he was the one who had told MG Putnam that we were "in good shape." Or maybe it was his job to make sure that we *were* "in good shape." Either way, it was obvious he had taken my comments personally. I decided to avoid that guy the rest of the evening.

After drinks we went into the general's personal mess. It was a private dining room separate from the larger mess hall. The walls were paneled in bamboo and thatching. The dining table was in the shape of a large First Air Cavalry Division patch and hand-carved in teak wood. Arranged around the table were place settings with individual place cards. Each place card had a little red two-star flag above our names. I was seated to the right of the general who sat at the "top" of the patch. MG Putnam formally introduced me to his staff officers, most of whom I had already met before dinner. My squadron commander, LTC. Carl M. Putnam (no relation) had also been invited.

The meal was pleasant, but I was uncomfortable surrounded by so many higher ranking officers. I was, after all, just a lowly WO1. The only other warrant officer there was the general's personal pilot. I was as much in awe of him as anyone else; he was a second-tour CW4. I had never met or even seen a CW4. Hell, I had never met or even seen a CW3.

After dinner, pictures were taken of all of us to mark the occasion. I got a few Polaroid pictures for my scrapbook. The evening ended with me being taken back to my hootch. I was tired; I had not recovered from the events of the last several days, so I went straight to bed.

The following day I was flown down to 3rd Field Hospital in Saigon to see an optometrist. He examined both eyes carefully and told me he believed that both eyes would eventually heal and go back to normal. I hoped that was true, and they were getting better every day.

Part V

Rest, Recovery, and Recuperation

Chapter Seventeen

I was getting close to the end of my week of rest that Cpt. Miller had promised me, when I became very sick. The symptoms felt similar to the flu but much worse: chills, nausea, vomiting, and diarrhea. I was taken to the local MED station, and they quickly decided I had malaria.

I said, "Malaria? Are you sure?"

"Yep," said the medic, "I'm sure. Have you been taking your malaria pills?"

"Of course," I said.

That was a lie; I did not know anyone who was taking the daily small white pills or the big red one on Mondays. Most of us in Apache already had diarrhea, and the pills made it worse, especially Monday's big red one.

"Well, you've got it; we'll be sending you to 3rd Field Hospital in Saigon."

I do not remember much about the next couple of days; I guess I was too sick. I do not even remember how I got there. I do remember being given some medicine for nausea. My eyes suddenly and violently crossed and rolled to the top of my head. I yelled out in pain, and the guy in the bed next to me leaned over me to see what was wrong. He took one look at me and ran to find a nurse. She took one look at me and ran to get something. She gave me some kind of a shot to counteract the nausea medicine, and my eyes slowly began to uncross and roll back to normal.

I said, "What happened?"

"Looks like you're allergic to Compazine," she said. "We gave you that for the nausea. Some people have a bad reaction to it."

"No shit!" I said sighing.

She laughed, and said, "Your eye muscles are relaxing already, and they'll be back to normal very soon; it will be better now."

There were no combat casualties on this ward; it was filled with guys with various diseases, many like me with malaria. I experienced episodes of high fever followed by the chills. This went on for several days. When I was going through the fever episodes, the nurses packed me in ice in my bed. When they were out of ice, they got me out of bed, and with one nurse under each arm carried me, complete with my IV bottle of quinine, to the shower where they held me under a blast of cold water for several minutes. That would be followed by more chills. Even under several blankets I was shaking so badly it hurt my jaw, and the wheels on the bed had to be locked to keep it from rolling across the floor.

I was on an IV bottle of quinine for ten days. It went with me everywhere. I was finally able to go to the latrine by myself in a wheel chair with a tall metal hook on the back to hold my IV bottle. I could also shower without any help. I hung my quinine bottle on one of the many hooks placed on the shower walls for that purpose.

The days passed, and I eventually got better. After ten days in the 3rd Field Hospital, ten days on an IV, I was told I would be going to the 6th Convalescent Center at Cam Ranh Bay.

I asked, "Can't I just go back to my unit, Doctor?"

"No, you're not well yet, but we need the beds here for folks who are a lot worse off than you. Get some rest and enjoy the beach."

A group of us were flown to Cam Ranh on an Air Force C-123. Apparently we did not rate a C-130. The C-123 was a twin engine cargo and troop transport being replaced by the newer four engine turboprop C-130. I hoped this was not one that had been used for spraying Agent Orange.

I always wondered why the Air Force painted all their planes in camouflage; they never sat anywhere out in the jungle. They were always based at large Air Force bases like Bien Hoa, and the enemy had no aircraft, at least not in South Vietnam. So,...what, the aircraft flies over and the enemy doesn't shoot at it because they think it's a bush?

We sat strapped in the nylon troop seats in our hospital gowns, literally with our asses hanging out. I am sure I was paranoid, but the whole time I thought, "If this aircraft goes down for some reason, I do not want to be running around in the jungle in a hospital gown." And, of course, we had no weapons. I felt naked; I almost was. I had been sleeping with my revolver under my pillow and my M16 under my cot since I had arrived in Apache. I had walked for four days in the jungle in Cambodia with my Smith & Wesson in my hand and cocked. I did not feel safe, and I did not like this at all.

It did not help looking out the window watching all the oil leaking down the sides of the radial engine nacelles; however, the weather was good and we arrived without incident.

Cam Ranh was right on the South China Sea roughly a third of the way up the coast of South Vietnam, a little less than 200 miles from Saigon. The sea was the most beautiful blue I had ever seen. I thought the Gulf of Mexico at Panama City, Florida, was beautiful, and it was, but this was really amazing.

The Convalescent Center was large, housed there with many other Army units and a large Air Force Base. We were bused from the air base over to the reception area for the hospital where we waited in a large room for a doctor to see us.

The brief examination would determine how sick we still were and how long they would keep us here.

Before he started, I said, "Doctor, I really am feeling much better, I would really like to go back to my unit."

He said, "Well, I'm glad to hear that you're feeling better. Let's have a look at you."

The examination did not last long; he poked hard low on both sides of my belly. He also briefly looked at my eyes, but I was there for the malaria, not the eyes, and there was not anything he could do for those anyway.

After the exam, he said, "I am sure you could use the rest, but if you still feel this way tomorrow, we'll see what we can do to get you back to your unit."

I thanked him. He was probably in his thirties, and we agreed to talk again the next day after I had had a meal, and hopefully, a good night's sleep.

An orderly led me down a long hallway, and eventually we arrived at my ward. As we walked through the door to the ward, I saw three guys all in hospital gowns sitting on a hospital bed playing cards. And there in the middle of them was Bob Spencer, my Ft. Rucker classmate, my hootch mate, and my best friend in Vietnam! I could not believe it! And I had just told the doctor that I wanted out of there as soon as possible!

I could not remember the last time I had seen Bob. We had made the move to Phuoc Vinh together and then were once again able to share a place to live. We started flying missions into Cambodia; by then he was back in the Lift Platoon, and shortly after that he came down with malaria, I had not seen him since. I was sure he did not know anything about me being shot down.

"Bob, what the hell are you doing here?" I yelled.

"Jeff, what the hell are *you* doing here?" he yelled.

That put an end to the card game and started a very long conversation of catching up. Like me, he had come down with malaria, but early in the Cambodian Operation. He had been sent to 3rd Field Hospital and eventually to Cam Ranh Bay. He had been here for a couple weeks already.

I gave him a short version of the "shoot down"; I would fill in the blanks and answer his dozens of questions later. I told him about my time in the jungle, and, of course, told him everything I knew about Kiser and Smoot. He was stunned. He had for a time also been a Scout pilot, Apache 14, but transferred back to the Lift Platoon and Hueys to get away from Cpt. Miller, which was the reason he had come over to Scouts in the first place. We could not believe we were here together in Cam Ranh.

He filled me in on life here in the hospital and what to expect. Like 3rd Field Hospital in Saigon, all the nurses here were American "round eyes" and to us good looking. Most seemed to be in their twenties and thirties. Their "highers" were, of course, older, but we never saw them. Bob explained that the meals would be brought to us in the ward but that we were basically free to come and go as we wished if we had the strength and felt like it. The beach was just down the road, and nurses who were not on duty could be found swimming and lying in the sun.

The day after I arrived, I tried to repair the damage done the previous day when I told the doctor on duty that I wanted to go back to my unit as soon as possible. When I was summoned for today's examination, it turned out to be a different doctor, and I quickly told him that his poking my spleen hurt a great deal. I was not lying; it did hurt. I had lied the day before when I told the doctor it did not; either way, that got me another two weeks in Cam Ranh.

Bob and I spent the days either playing cards in the ward or on the beach eating shrimp. Most days and especially nights, we played cards. As beautiful as the South China Sea was, we found out pretty quickly the beach was too damn hot. Some of our friends could not leave the ward or did not feel like it. The hospital ward was, after all, air conditioned.

We spent every night playing Spades or Hearts, but no Poker because no one had any money. There was a small black-and-white TV in the corner, and we listened and watched Armed Forces Network while we played cards. Every night they showed the same re-runs of *Hawaii Five-O*. There for a while they showed the same episode every night. One of those episodes with Wo Fat as the Chinese bad guy. We saw it so many times that we memorized the lines, and each of us spoke someone's part as we played cards.

Even though the show itself got old, we always enjoyed hearing the theme song by The Ventures.

Like my ward at 3rd Field Hospital, this ward had no battle casualties. Everyone here had either a tropical disease, most of them malaria, or a venereal disease. The guy in the bunk next to me, Ed Wilson, had gonorrhea. Damn, I felt bad for him! He was a great guy, and every day at about the same time the nurse would come in with a huge needle. I did not know what the gauge was on that thing, but it was big.

The nurse would say that she was sorry, but that it was time again for his shot. Ed would roll over on this side towards me, pull his pajama bottoms down to expose the cheek of his butt, and hug his pillow. He never said a word, but when the needle went in, *all the way*, his face just burst out in perspiration. Damn, that must hurt. He got that shot every day for, I think, two weeks. I wondered if she was worth it.

The nurses were great to us, but we quickly found out that even the most average-looking nurses were in high demand and could hold out for the best-looking men of the highest ranks. Average-looking girls were dating guys who would never have paid them any attention back in the States. Two average-looking WO1s with no money did not have any chance here. That did not mean we didn't try, but we didn't have any luck.

The nurses lived in groups of American made trailers as did the highest-ranking officers. The trailers had been brought over from the United States just for that purpose. We could see lots of men visiting the nurse's trailers and vice versa. There did not seem to be any reason to hide the extracurricular activities; everyone was a long way from home. Bob and I were also a long way from home, and we were envious.

After a couple more weeks of living in what many would consider paradise (except for the lack of female companionship), Bob and I were both discharged at the same time. We were given passes to catch a flight down south and taken to the air base. There we were told by Flight Operations that there were no seats for us on flights going anywhere south and probably would not be for several days. We went back to the hospital and asked what we were supposed to do and where we were supposed to stay. It was no surprise that the hospital could not put us up in our old ward. They recommended a group of transient quarters not far from the hospital until we could get out of Cam Ranh. We moved into a vacant transient hootch and tried to figure out what to do.

Surely our unit would be notified that we had been discharged, and every day we did not show up back in Apache, not counting a reasonable amount of travel time, we would be considered AWOL. We were both new to Vietnam and to the ways of the Army; we did not know what to do or how to contact anyone. I was sure a seasoned NCO would know exactly what to do and who to contact, but we did not. Every day, or every other day, we would travel to the air base to talk to flight operations to try to get a flight to somewhere down south. Anywhere down south, no luck. This went on for two more weeks. This was so crazy; we were trapped in paradise. I thought of all the poor bastards that would have given anything to be in this same situation.

We stayed in the hootch out of the sun sleeping and reading paperbacks most of the day. It was very hot, and the hootch was not air conditioned. We had gotten spoiled quickly in the hospital wards, first in Saigon and then in Cam Ranh. We ate at the hospital mess and lay on the beach in the evenings. Sometimes we went back over to the old ward and played cards with the friends we had made there.

Finally we were able to get on a flight to Long Binh. From there we caught a ride on a Huey to Bien Hoa. We made our way to the 1st Air Cav Division "Rear" (or what had been 1st Air Cav Division "Rear"); there was almost no one there. We were informed that while we had been in the hospital, the First Air Cavalry Division had "stood down," meaning they had packed up and left Vietnam, part of President Nixon's promise to de-escalate the war. Many, if not most of the units that made up the 1st Air Cav, were distributed to other divisions. So many that we later wondered who exactly went back to Ft. Hood (Texas). We joked about it; maybe it was only two guys carrying the flags.

The 1st Squadron of the 9th Cavalry had been given to the 1st Aviation Brigade. We belonged to them now. The 1st Aviation Brigade was already much larger than a normal brigade, and now it included the 1st of the 9th complete with the newly formed "F" Troop.

"So where are they?" I asked.

"Who?" asked the sergeant.

"The 1st Aviation Brigade," I said.

"They're all over," he said.

"Where is the 1st of the 9th?" I asked. I did not feel well. I was not over the malaria, and I was getting impatient.

"You'll have to ask the 1st Aviation Brigade," he replied.

"Look," Bob said, "Who do we talk to to find our unit?"

It was probably good that I had no weapon. We eventually learned that it was believed that the 1st of the 9th "Rear" was located at a place called Di An (pronounced Zeon) southwest of Bien Hoa and north of Saigon. It was not explained to us that Di An was not spelled with a "Z" as it was pronounced, but rather with a "D" so we continued to search all the maps we could find looking for a Zi An or possibly a Ze An, with no success. Finally someone showed us on a map how Di An was spelled and where it was.

Chapter Eighteen

Bob and I finally showed up at Squadron something like five or six weeks after I had come down with malaria. Bob had been gone even longer. We were directed to the location of Apache Troop and reported to the duty officer in the orderly room. We told him who we were and where we had been. The place looked deserted inside and out.

The duty officer, a 1Lt. Bradley, a new guy who neither one of us knew, said, "Oh, yeah, Mr. Houser and Mr. Spencer, malaria, I was keeping an eye out for you two, but we really didn't expect you guys back for another couple of weeks."

Bob and I looked at each other, and I am sure we both thought the same thing: "You have got to be shitting me. We could have stayed in Cam Ranh another couple of weeks?!"

"Where is everybody?" I asked.

The lieutenant informed us that almost all of Apache was located at Tay Ninh West, and that we should go up there as soon as we could get a ride. The troop was still operating inside Cambodia, but instead of living at Phuoc Vinh and staging out of Loc Ninh every day, we were living and working out of Tay Ninh West since it was so close to the border.

Tay Ninh was a major city about 50 miles northwest of Saigon. Tay Ninh West was the airfield we would be working out of just to the north and west of Tay Ninh. Tay Ninh was roughly 45 miles due west of Phuoc Vinh and about 45 or 50 miles southwest of Loc Ninh.

The strategic importance of the area was that it was so close to the Cambodian Border. Tay Ninh actually lies north and west of a piece of Cambodia that juts deep into South Vietnam dangerously close to Saigon. The well-known areas of the "Parrot's Beak" and the "Angle's Wing," so named because that is what they look like on the map, are actually south and east of Tay Ninh.

Cu Chi, famous for its hundreds of miles of tunnels, was nearby to the southeast. It was believed by Army Intelligence that some tunnels went all the way to Saigon and into the city. The "Iron Triangle" was also nearby; east of Tay Ninh and north of Saigon, it had always been a communist stronghold, first by the Viet Minh against the French, and now by the Viet Cong against the government of South Vietnam and the Americans. It was assumed by MACV (Military Assistance Command Vietnam) and USARV (United States Army Vietnam) that if North Vietnam ever felt they could conquer the south with a conventional ground war attack, these places would hold the key to the success of taking Saigon.

To the northeast of Tay Ninh a few miles lay Nui Ba Den, the "Black Virgin" Mountain. Like Nui Ba Ra at Song Be, Nui Ba Den was the only mountain in the area and was a very distinctive landmark for a pilot in daylight and good weather. It was, however, much larger than Nui Ba Ra. Also, like the mountain at Song Be, there was a small group of Americans operating a radio-relay station on the very top of the mountain. The VC controlled the sides of the mountain complete with a complex system of caves all over it. The only way in or out for the guys on top of the mountain was by helicopter. So, again like Nui Ba Ra, we Americans controlled the top and the land around the base, but the VC controlled the sides.

While we were together in the hospital, Bob and I discussed our future and Scouts. I told Bob in one of those late night discussions that I was ready to go back to Scouts, and that was what I intended to do as soon as we got back. I was the most senior Scout pilot now in Apache Troop and had been even before the malaria and the hospital. I helped train Cpt. Miller, my new platoon leader. I told Bob that I probably didn't really have a choice anyway.

Bob thought I did have a choice, after all, Scouts was voluntary, and because I had been in well over six months, plus being shot down, he thought I could get out any time I wanted.

In theory, participation in Scouts was voluntary for six months, that is, pilots were only expected to stay for six months. In reality, most pilots never left Scouts once they were in it. Ty Graham, "Captain America," left Scouts to go to a Cobra transition and came back as a "Gun" pilot. Bob left to go back to the "Lift" to get away from Cpt. Miller. But for most, once they were in Scouts, they never left until the end of their tour (or until they were badly injured or killed).

The six-month idea really did not seem to mean anything. And anyway, in spite of everything, I liked Scouts. I liked the mission, I liked the OH-6, I felt respected, especially now, and I felt at home there.

Bob told me that he was really considering coming back to Scouts himself and reclaiming his call sign of "Apache 14," regardless of Ace Miller being "White." He said he really liked the Lift platoon and the guys in it, but that he missed flying the Scout mission and flying the OH-6.

I said, "Bob, Cambodia is really not a good time to come back to Scouts; you might want to wait until the Cambodian mission is over. On the other hand, Cpt. Miller has been awfully nice to me after being shot down; maybe he's changed."

"Well," he said, "he knows that MG Putnam likes you, and you could go see him pretty much any time you want. But that doesn't change the way he feels about me."

"Yeah, maybe."

"And," he reminded me, "remember what LTC Putnam (no relation to MG Putnam) told us in that formation we had just before we went into Cambodia? When he "asked" us for 100% participation in what he said would only last three to five days, we went across the border the last week of February, and it's now the end of April. It may never be over."

"Well," I said, "it's, of course, up to you. But you're more likely to survive this shit in "Lift."

We found out at Di An that while we were in the hospital we had lost more of our friends.

1Lt. Larry Lilly had been killed in Cambodia the 17th of March, a week after I went down. He had been the front seat co-pilot/gunner in a Cobra with Apache 28, David "Doc" Schweitzer, when they were shot down. They took hits trying to protect ARVN troops that had already been inserted into an LZ and were now just inside the tree line of the clearing. They were being attacked by the NVA who had them outnumbered and were trying to surround them. Doc and Larry landed upright in a successful autorotation into the same LZ. They both got out of the aircraft and started to run to the Huey that had followed them in to pick them up.

The cockpit doors on a Cobra open in opposite directions: the front seat co-pilot door opens on the left, the backseat AC door opens on the right. So the guys were separated immediately, having gotten out on opposite sides of the aircraft. While they were running to the Huey, Larry was seen to have taken at least two hits in the back; he fell there. Doc made it to the Huey, and they lifted off.

For a while our people still had radio contact with the ARVNs who reported that they had recovered Larry's body and that he was dead. They also reported that they were surrounded. That was the last radio contact we had.

Since the U.S. Government never saw the body (we never recovered it), Larry was "officially" listed as missing, even though we knew he was dead.

CW2 Paul Foti and 1Lt Don Osborn were also dead. Apache 25, Paul Foti, and his co-pilot Don Osborn were flying as my "high bird" (Cobra protection) the day I was shot down. They had risked their lives to make many low slow passes down the river looking for us before they finally decided that we were dead. They took so many hits and were shot up so badly that they had to make a precautionary landing at Snuol. It was determined by maintenance the aircraft would have to be "retrograded," sent back to the States to be rebuilt.

On the 23rd of March they were on a weather mission in the vicinity of Snuol when they stopped responding to radio calls. They were alone at the time since the purpose of the flight was to determine if the weather was good enough to launch "Pink Teams" (a White Platoon Scout and a Red Platoon Cobra) for a time they just seemed to disappear.

The wreckage of the aircraft was eventually found by the ARVNs not far from Snuol. It took awhile but eventually it was determined that their aircraft, AH-1G #68-15111, had been hit by "friendly" artillery fire. We had no American artillery units on the ground in Cambodia, and it was too far away for our artillery inside Vietnam to reach there, so it had to be ARVN artillery.

Whether they did not contact artillery to see who was firing and where, or whether the ARVNs did not tell anyone they were firing, no one seemed to know. Paul and Don were gone.

Cambodia was taking its toll. It was about this time that I found out through the "grapevine", since they were not in the 1st of the 9th or even the 1st Air Cavalry Division, that two of my classmates, WO1 Carl Nacca and WO1 Hugh Pettit had both been killed.

Back on the 20th of February, Carl was in the front seat of a Cobra attacking a .51 cal gun emplacement when his aircraft was hit, crashed, and burned. He and his AC (aircraft commander) 1Lt. John Hunter were both killed.

More recently, on the 10th of April, Hugh was the AC on a MEDEVAC mission when his Huey crashed. No one seemed to have any information as to what happened. Once again, fine young men, America's best, gone.

Chapter Nineteen

Cpt. Miller found me and said that he wanted to talk to me. Bob and I were sharing a small hootch that we had found unoccupied, barely enough room for the two of us. Cpt. Miller and I stood outside; we did not have room inside. He said he had made some changes while I was in the hospital.

"Mr. Houser, it's good to see you back. What had you planned to do now?" he asked.

"What do you mean, Sir?" I asked.

"What do you want to do?"

"I didn't think I had a choice, but either way, I want to continue in Scouts."

"Well, that's what I want to talk to you about," he said, "You have certainly done your part for Scouts. Did you realize that you have become the most senior Scout pilot in the troop?"

"Yes, sir, I know that."

"Well, I really think that you've used up about all the luck you have, and I have another job for you," he said.

"Another job, what do you mean?" I asked. "I don't want to go to Lift."

"No, this isn't a flying job," he said. "This is a desk job."

"What, …a desk job?"

"Yes, we need a liaison officer to work with the ARVNs."

"A liaison officer, I don't know anything about that."

"Sure you do; you're an aviator. You're an experienced combat pilot particularly in Scouts. But you've flown Lift missions, and you certainly know all about the Gun Platoon and how they operate. That's what they need over there, somebody that knows how we do things and can work with the ARVN command. There are a lot of things about working with us that they still do not understand."

"Do I have a choice in this?" I asked.

"Yes, but I really believe you should take the offer. You've done your part, Houser. Think about it. I'm trying to do you a favor here."

I thought about it. I thought about it all night. Maybe he was right; maybe I *had* used up all my luck. I told him the next day that I would do it.

The ARVN headquarters was about a half mile away. For a while I walked back and forth every day. I was still living with Bob. Then the American colonel I actually worked for decided that he wanted me to live over there with them. There was a small group of American "advisers" living there in what at one time had been an office building, and I moved in with two of them. They had taken over one of the offices and made it into their quarters. There was more than enough room for the three of us. It was actually the first time since being in Vietnam, other than the hospital stays, that I was living in a real brick and mortar building.

It was the most comfortable living conditions I had had; it even had a carpeted floor. The three of us got along very well. I helped them redo the office and build a small bar. Actually, there were four of us; we had a dog named Ralph living with us. No one knew who Ralph belonged to or who fed him, but he seemed to like living with us. We did not see him all day, and then he would come wandering in in the evening and stay with us every night.

I was assigned an interpreter, a South Vietnamese soldier named Sgt. Tam, and he went everywhere with me. He was probably in his mid-20s. Sometimes I needed an interpreter to talk *with* him. Like young American men who came from families with no money and no connections, Vietnamese males were also conscripted. Unlike American draftees who served two years, Vietnamese males were in the army for the duration. Tam was very likeable, but I spent any free time I had with the American advisers, and sometimes I walked back over to the Apache living area.

I visited Bob one time after a bad rain to find that the hootch we had shared together was completely flooded. Like a lot of other G.I.s, we had bought a plastic mat to keep from walking on the bare dirt floor in bare feet. The mat had floated right out the front of the hootch; we did not have a door. I did not want to remind Bob that I was now living in a carpeted office.

Part of my liaison job was to monitor the radios in a small room in the ARVN TOC. I listened in on my Apache Troop frequencies following their missions and explaining to the American colonel if need be what was going on.

I was doing that on the 7th of May when 1Lt. (Frank) Walt Bengtson, a friend of mine, and his crew were shot down not far from where I had gone down back in March. It was believed that they were also hit by an RPG (rocket propelled grenade) as I had been. They crashed and immediately burned. Walt, WO1 David Meyer, and their door gunner, SP4 Larry Rothel, were all killed in the crash. I listened helplessly as our Hueys and Cobras tried to get to them and help them. There was nothing that could be done. Eventually we were able to recover the bodies.

Finally, in June, the Cambodian Campaign ended. Apache Troop, along with the rest of the 1st of the 9th, stood down. We were to be given back to the 1st Air Cavalry Division now back at Ft. Hood, Texas. I was no longer needed as liaison officer so I moved back over to be with the rest of Apache.

We had lost a lot of good people in the last four months and a lot of aircraft, mainly OH-6 LOHs.

How many people and aircraft had we lost now just in my troop?

Apache 16, WO1 (Walter) Bob Smith, "Smitty," had been shot down and did a complete forward end-over-end somersault into the trees in their bird. Smitty and his crew were uninjured, other than minor cuts and bruises, and picked up within minutes.

Apache 11, CW2 Bob Long, had been shot down and suffered some injuries. They were also picked up quickly. Both aircraft were total loses. Kiser and Smoot had been lost in 412; there was still nothing new on Curtis Smoot. Walt Bengtson, David Meyer, and Larry Rothel had all been killed in 679. Again, both of those aircraft were a total loss.

We lost another great guy and a great Scout door gunner, Sgt. Monty Harbin, before we ever even got into Cambodia. On the night before the invasion, the 22nd of February, Monty and a group of our most experienced door gunners and observers were badly injured in a terrible explosion in our ammo "dump," a large CONEX box. This is where we kept all of the ammunition, grenades, and explosives for the Scout Platoon.

Grenades arrive from the manufacturer in a wooden crate. The wooden box is packed with grenades individually protected in cardboard tubes. The grenades are removed from the tubes and placed in an ammo box that will be placed on each aircraft. Each torque/door gunner had a preference as to the types of grenades that he would want to use, or that he knew his pilot preferred, and he would pack his ammo box appropriately. Fragmentation grenades, concussion grenades, white phosphorus grenades, incendiary grenades, several different colors of smoke grenades -- all had a different purpose.

As Monty removed one of the white phosphorus grenades, known in the trade as a "Willie Pete," the "spoon" flipped, setting the fuse. As long as the grenade is in its cardboard tube, the spoon cannot possibly flip. Once it is removed from the tube, the "pin" keeps the spoon from flipping. This grenade obviously had no pin. It had come from the factory with no pin! In the pre-dawn darkness of the CONEX box lit by one hanging light bulb, Monty did not notice that it had no pin until it was already out of the tube. The spring-loaded spoon made a very distinctive sound when it flipped; he tried to run with it and get it out of the CONEX, but he did not have time. All of them in there were horribly burned. Monty died the next day of suffocation; his lungs were scorched.

Those were just the Scouts that we lost in Cambodia or because of it. I had just called Monty's wife at his request a few weeks earlier (I was home on leave) to tell her that Monty was fine. They had a new baby.

We had also lost 1Lt. Larry Lilly, CW2 Paul Foti, and 1Lt. Donald Osborn in their two Cobras, and both of those were total losses. Needless-to-say, all these aircraft could be replaced; these heroic young men, our friends, could not.

Thankfully, we had not lost anyone or any Hueys from the Lift Platoon.

We quickly moved out of Di An and once again moved back to Phuoc Vinh. We were now in relatively comfortable individual rooms. I was tired of moving. Several of my belongings had been lost in the move from Phuoc Vinh to Di An while I was in the hospital. I never knew who had packed my stuff for the move, but I ended up losing a lot of my personal possessions. Among them: the glass in which Col. Truong had given me a beer with the peaches in the ARVN bunker at Snuol. That was a prized possession.

The partitions between the individual rooms stopped a few inches above the floor, I suppose, so that the air could circulate. But that left a way for the water beetles to get from room to room. These water beetles were much larger than any I had ever seen in the United States, big nasty-ass-looking things with big pincers. I would chase them back through the wall (Bob lived on the other side) with a spray can of Right Guard deodorant and a cigarette lighter.

You had to be careful not to burn yourself or blow up the can, but if you held the can just right, you could ignite the spray like a flame thrower and chase the ugly bastards back under the wall. They would run for their lives; damn they could move! Before long you could make out the roar sound of someone on the other side of the wall, usually Bob, doing the same thing, and sure enough, back they would come. I always checked my boots before I put them on, but I had been doing that for a long time.

One by one our guys were leaving and either going back to the States or being sent to another unit in Vietnam, depending on how much time they had in-country. Every day there were less of us and still I had no orders. I now had enough time in Vietnam to go home even though I did not quite have a full twelve month tour. I went to Cpt. Miller and once again he came through for me. He made a middle of the night (in Vietnam) phone call to Warrant Officer Branch in the Pentagon. I was too new to the Army to even know there was such a thing as Warrant Officer Branch. I listened as he talked to whoever was on the other end of the line in Washington; he wanted to know why I did not have orders yet.

"Where are Mr. Houser's orders?" He asked firmly.

Because of his call Branch cut DEROS orders on me right away. I would be going home.

It seemed like so long ago when Cpt. Ace Miller and his buddy Cpt. Al Ferrea seemed to get such great enjoyment giving Bob and I a rough time. Now they could not have been nicer.

Part VI

The Way Home

Chapter Twenty

The last time I had been home was just before the Cambodian Operation. Bob and I had decided to put in for a seven-day R & R in Australia. The Rest and Relaxation (or recuperation) policy was a little ambiguous, but the idea was to allow guys to leave their unit for a few days to unwind and have a good time.

You had a choice of taking an in-country (usually three days) or a seven-day out-of-the-country R & R. Out-of-country R & Rs supposedly had a minimum requirement of how much time you had spent in Vietnam. Priority was to be given to the men who had served the longest without a break. Sydney, Australia; Bangkok, Thailand; Tokyo, Japan; and, of course, Hawaii were the first choices. There were several others. Yes, Hawaii was included, but you were forbidden to leave Hawaii to go all the way to CONUS (Continental United States). The seven days counted against your leave time; the three day in-country did not.

Bob and I put in the necessary paperwork, and we were surprised to learn that not only had we both been approved for the R & R but for the same seven-day period! We would travel together to Sydney; the girls there were English speaking, white girls with “round eyes.” Whether it was true or not, we had often been told that the girls in Sydney outnumbered the guys 3 to 1. We were going to Sydney.

Not long after we received our approval notice, we found out that for the first time the Pentagon was going to allow a 14 day leave back to CONUS. The Pentagon had never allowed that before (except Emergency Leave) with good reason: they were afraid you would not come back. Some probably did not.

Bob and I weighed the possibility of a 14 day leave back home against the seven-day R & R that had already been approved; we could not do both. A chance to see your family and friends again, possibly for the last time, against probably a really good time in Australia. Both would count against our leave time, but of the 14 day leave back to the States, four days (at least for me going to Indiana) would be lost in travel. So I would be charged for 14 days and only really have 10 days at home, assuming no missed flights, cancellations, or other glitches.

Also the cost of the airline tickets was to be considered; this would be on us. Bob was going to California, but I was going all the way to Indiana. We had three options: we could try to find a military flight going somewhere near our destination and fly "Space-A" (Space Available) for free, we could try to fly Military Reserve on a commercial airline, usually around two thirds the price of a regular ticket, or we could pay the regular full price for the ticket on a commercial airline and be guaranteed a seat.

Flying free on a U.S. Air Force flight sounded good, but there was always the chance of the flight being diverted; a flight scheduled for San Francisco could get diverted to Anchorage, Alaska. You never knew. *They* never knew. Flying Military Reserve on a commercial airline meant the possibility of being "bumped" by someone with a full-price ticket. I decided I could not take a chance on either of those; if I was approved for the leave, I would book a full-price 2nd class round-trip ticket. I would literally be going half way around the world and back. Literally, the time difference between Vietnam and Indiana was twelve hours.

We eventually received word that both of our requests for leave had been approved, but not for the same time period. He would leave two weeks before me, and we would pass each other somewhere on his way back. I continued to fly missions hoping that something would not happen to me before I was able to go home. The days went slowly but really without incident, well… normal Scout missions. Finally in early February Bob was due back any time, and I was due to leave.

I had not told my mother or anyone at home that I would be getting a two-week leave. This was the Army: too many things could go wrong and screw this up. I did not want to disappoint her. I would be crushed, but I did not want her to be. I did not want her to know anything about it until I was knocking on the front door.

My leave orders did come through, and I left for the "The World." I had to go through all of the hassle of getting from Phuoc Vinh to Bien Hoa to Tan Son Nhut Air Base at Saigon, but I caught my military charter flight filled with English speaking American flight attendants with very short skirts. I was on my way from Saigon to Yokota, Japan, to San Francisco to Indianapolis. Actual flight time was probably 18 hours or so, but with the refueling stop at Yokota outside Tokyo, switching carriers at San Francisco, and the delay in between flights, the trip was a full 24 hours.

The closer I got to home, the better I felt. I actually felt like I *was* home when we touched down in California. I arrived in Indianapolis at night. It was February and cold, and I was dressed in TWs (Tropical Weights): a short sleeve, thin material, warm weather dress uniform. I had no jacket or coat. I did not care; I was in Indiana in the United States.

I tried to rent a car, but Hertz would not let me unless I had a credit card. Neither would any of the other rental agencies. I was 21; my birthday had been in January, and I had the cash. It did not matter; they all had the same policy: no credit card, no rental car. Shit. I had just come half way around the world and now I needed to go another 60 miles, and I could not get there.

The girl at the desk was sympathetic but said she could not do anything.

I said, "You've got to be shitting me; I just came 12,000 miles! I just need to go another 60!"

"I'm so sorry," she said, "but there's nothing I can do."

"Any ideas?" I asked.

"Well, not really. You could get a taxi. I don't know what that would cost, and those guys over there who keep looking at you run a limousine service. I don't have any idea what that would cost either. I'm sorry."

I had noticed two guys in black suits staring at me like vultures on the hunt, but I had not really paid any attention to them. They looked more like they had a hearse waiting than a limo. I asked them what it would cost to take me to Connersville, and just as I figured, it was prohibitive.

"No," I said. "There's no way in hell that I'm going to pay that."

The one guy said, "Well, that's the only way you're going to get there, son."

"I'm not your son, and fuck you, I'll take a cab."

Meantime the girl from the car rental had heard all this and motioned me back over to her counter.

"Where did you say you wanted to go?" she asked.

"Connersville. It's about 60 miles southeast."

"Is that anywhere near Shelbyville?"

"Well, sort of. They're both on highway 44. Connersville is probably another 35 miles or so to the east of Shelbyville."

"Well, we've got a guy working in the back here, Mike, who lives in Shelbyville, and he will be getting off work here in a little bit. I thought maybe you could work something out with him."

"Sure, thank you so much. Let me talk to him."

In a few minutes a burly guy a little younger than I am came out from the back and said hello.

"You're wanting to go to Connersville?" he asked.

"Right," I said.

"Well, I can get you as far as Shelbyville; that's where I'm going."

"What would it take to get you to take me all the way?"

"Well, I don't know. That would run me awfully late getting back."

"What would it take?"

"Gas money?"

"Sure."

He dropped me off in front of my mom's house (our house) in Connersville. In return, I had filled his tank with gas and bought him a case of beer. Seemed fair.

There was a car in the driveway that I did not recognize. I walked to the front door and knocked. My mom answered the door with a shocked look on her face. We hugged tightly.

"What, ……Why, ……How, ……?"

"I know, Mom." I said, and I explained to her why I had not told her ahead of time about my intended leave. She saw Mike pull away, and I explained to her how all of that came about.

"But I could have picked you up," she said.

"I know, Mom," I said, and I told her again why I did not tell her.

"But you could have called from Indianapolis," she said.

"I thought I might have to, but I wanted to surprise you."

"You did," she said, laughing but still shocked and almost in tears.

She then introduced me to "Jim," the fella she had been dating. He was a supervisor at Philco-Ford where my mom was a secretary in the maintenance department. She explained to me that "Jim" was on his dinner break at work and had stopped by for coffee.

The both of us were so excited to see each other that neither of us paid much attention to her guest, and he eventually stormed out, not finishing his coffee and not saying goodbye.

"Mom, what was that all about?" I asked. "I wasn't trying to be rude, but it's not like we see each other all the time. I haven't seen you since August."

"I know; don't worry about it. Sometimes he's like that. I am so glad to have you home," and we hugged again.

I was home for the next several days, and that first meeting with Jim Davis pretty much set the tone for our relationship over the brief course of my leave. Thankfully I did not have to see him every day, but most nights he would stop by for coffee on his "break." Sometimes I would be there, and often I was not. My mother wanted me to meet his family, not a good sign. He was a widower with four children, (two boys and two girls), and I was convinced he was looking for a mother for them. They were terrified of him. I found out later their mother had committed suicide. I thought I knew why.

Besides seeing my mother and little brother, I spent time with some of my friends, especially Sam Hankins and Danny Sizemore. I missed seeing Ron Larmore; he was away at college at Ball State University in Muncie. Leon Blakley was in the Navy somewhere. I saw a couple of girls. I talked to Peggy (Sam's younger sister), absolutely beautiful and just as sweet as ever; we promised to write each other.

I visited my grandmother and my aunt in Richmond. I saw my dad in New Paris, Ohio. The time went by very quickly. Before I knew it, it was time to go back.

I decided to leave a day early. I had seen everyone I wanted to see, and Bob Spencer's mother had arranged for me to meet a girl in Los Angeles who had been writing to me. Her mother and Bob's mother worked together, so they had arranged it with Chris's mother that I could stay there a day and night and have Chris show me around LA. I decided to do it.

My mother and my grandmother took me to the airport. I think it was harder leaving for Vietnam this time than it had been before. At least I knew where I was going and what I would be doing; maybe that's why it was worse. But I never even considered *not* going back.

I arrived at Los Angeles International Airport, something I had seen so many times on TV and in the movies. The iconic flying saucer-looking building standing on four legs could not be missed. I was told that it was a restaurant. I walked down the endless hallway and finally found a down escalator. There at the bottom of the escalator looking up was a beautiful blonde-haired blue-eyed girl, probably 20. Just breathtaking. My first thought was, "Wouldn't that be something if that was Chris?" It turned out it was!

"Jeff?"

"Chris?"

"You made it," Chris said.

"Yes," I said. "I did, and so did you."

"Well, I didn't have as far to go."

We both laughed; she spent what was left of the day and almost all night showing me Los Angeles. We went to Hollywood, drove down Hollywood Boulevard past Grauman's Chinese Theatre, Westwood, UCLA campus, Marina del Rey, Santa Monica Beach, and, of course, miles of driving along the ocean. I had a great time, and I think she did, too. Nothing romantic -- just two young people having fun. Once again, it was difficult to leave.

Chapter Twenty-One

My orders finally arrived, thanks to Cpt. Miller, and I left Phuoc Vinh for what I hoped would be the last time. I was sent back to the REPO DEPO at Bien Hoa. After three days there, having been told every day that I could not wear my Cav hat and refusing to take it off, we were bused to Tan Son Nhut Air Base on the outskirts of Saigon. There we waited for our flight back to "The World."

I had traded a refrigerator for a Chicom (Chinese Communist) 7.62 mm SKS rifle. It was semi-automatic and foreign-made, so I could legally register the weapon as a war trophy and take it back to the United States. The Department of Defense would allow you to take two weapons home, either two rifles, or two handguns, or one of each, the stipulation being that they could not be of U.S. origin, and they could not be fully automatic.

I had obtained two AK-47s during my tour, one with a folding stock and one with the normal wooden stock. The AK with the folding stock was particularly nice to carry in the Scout bird; with the stock folded, it was shorter than my M-16, roughly the length of a CAR-15, and I fastened it on the map light between the seats. I traded with the "Blues" for captured 7.62 mm ammunition for it. Both of the AKs were fully automatic, so I could not take them home.

I also had traded a flight suit to one of the advisers I was living with at Di An for a.45 cal M-3 tankers "grease gun" that had been floating around the Black Market since probably the 1940s or 1950s. It did not matter to the Army how long it had been out of their control; it was of American origin, so it still belonged to them, and it was also fully automatic, so I could not take that home either. I sold or traded these fully automatic weapons before I left Vietnam. In fact, Curtis Smoot ended up with the AK with the full wooden stock. I held on to the other

AK with the folding stock until shortly before the Cambodian Campaign.

Just before I left, I had a chance to buy a Chicom Type 54 pistol with a holster and an extra magazine. I should have bought that, but I didn't. It seemed like a lot of money at the time.

There were 200 and some of us waiting to board the "Freedom Bird" on the ramp at Ton Son Nhut. There was no order of rank, and I somehow managed to be the sixth person in line. I had a major on one side of me and a colonel on the other. We had been through some form of security or customs in the terminal, and we were now in single file in the hot sun waiting to board. I was standing there with my Cav hat on and a single carry-on bag in my hand; I had already checked my SKS rifle and my bags. We were all anxious to get on the plane and get in the air when we were stopped by MPs who wanted one last look at our belongings before we got on the plane.

I had placed my Buck knife in my shaving kit that was in a small carry-on bag. The Buck knife that my dad had given me before leaving for Vietnam. The Buck knife that I had with me the whole time I was in Vietnam. The Buck knife that I carried with me the four days I was on the ground in Cambodia. One by one the MPs went through our carry-on.

The one MP, a sergeant E5, pulled my knife out of my shaving kit and said, "Well, what's this?"

I said, "What do you mean?"

"Well, this folding knife is not allowed," he said.

"What do you mean it's not allowed?"

"The blade is longer than is authorized."

Now I had just checked in a rifle with a 12-inch bayonet fastened on it, and no one said a word. When I went home on leave in February, I took with me a VC knife that Monty Harbin had given me; it had an

11-inch blade. Going through customs in California, the agent only asked what it was and I told him my door gunner killed the guy and gave me the knife; he put it back in my bag.

"Well, what is authorized?" I asked the sergeant.

He laid the open blade across his four fingers and said, "This is too long."

"This is bullshit!" I said.

"Well, if you want to stay and argue about it, *Sir,* you can, but you will miss this flight."

There it was. I could either stay there and ask for his OIC (Officer In Charge) and miss my flight or acquiesce and lose my knife. I looked at the line of over 200 guys waiting in the hot sun wondering what the holdup was. It was obvious what I had to do. I was not going to miss this flight that I had waited a year to be on. I also did not want these other guys waiting any longer in the sun. It was clear to me that this MP son-of-a-bitch, who had probably never been in combat, never had ducked anything other than a flying beer bottle in a bar in Saigon, was going to keep my knife for himself. Dirty low-life son-of-a-bitch.

I wondered what he would tell his family and his children when they asked him about what he did in "The War."

"Well, son, I stole things from soldiers who were leaving Vietnam after they had served a year in actual combat there."

I boarded the plane.

Chapter Twenty-Two

I sat with an Army infantry captain named John Montgomery and exchanged small talk. He asked me what happened back on the ramp before boarding, and I told him about it. He could not believe it either. He noticed my wings and my ribbons, and eventually he asked me what I had done on my tour. I told him.

He said, "Well, that explains it."

I said, "What do you mean?"

"Your awards. That's what these other guys are looking at and wondering about. I see you were in the CAV and now you tell me you flew Scouts, so that explains the Purple Heart, the Bronze Stars, and I'm not sure what that is."

"Which?"

"That," pointing to my DFC.

"Distinguished Flying Cross."

"Oh, sure, OK. Some of these guys probably think you bought a bunch of those on the "Black Market" to impress your family and friends when you get home. Some assholes do that, you know."

"Yeah, I know, but I didn't."

"Oh, I believe you. I read a story in *Stars and Stripes* a while back about a Scout pilot who was shot down in Cambodia and was alone on the ground for four days in the jungle before he walked out. Four days! He was in the CAV."

"Yeah, I saw that."

"You don't happen to know him, do you?"

"Yes, actually, I used to know him."

The captain of the Boeing 707 came on the intercom and announced that we had just cleared Vietnamese airspace and, of course, there was a great applause and yells of delight. This was going to be the fourth time I had crossed the Pacific Ocean. I still had not figured out the International Date Line: going one way you lose a day, going the other way you gain a day. Damn, that is confusing.

I had hoped I would get to see Hawaii, at least from the air, but once again we were not stopping there. From the west coast both times we had flown the northern route: Alaska and then to Japan. Going east we flew to Japan but then straight to San Francisco. Being a pilot, I figured it must have something to do with the difference in winds?

As with the three times before that I had been to Yokota, we were only on the ground an hour, but we were made to leave the plane. I spent the hour stretching my legs and looking through the various vendors' shops. I found a guy who could engrave things while you waited, so I bought a new Zippo lighter to replace the one I had lost in Cambodia. (Somewhere along the way during my E & E (escape and evasion) in Cambodia, I had lost my Zippo. Probably bending over to drink water). I had him engrave my name, my call sign, and my unit on it with the understanding that I could not wait long. He finished the lighter with time to spare. He did a great job and all by hand with a tool: no machines, nothing electric.

Once again we boarded, this time for the last and longest leg. Cpt. Montgomery and I talked some, but most of the time I slept. I would look out at the ocean for while, amazed at how big it was, talk a little, eat and drink something, then go back to sleep. I would sleep two or three hours, wake up, look at the ocean, look at the pretty flight attendants, and fall back asleep. Every time I woke up, we were still over the Pacific. That's a lot of ocean.

I was awake to hear the airline captain announce that we had entered American airspace, and once again there was uproar on board the aircraft. We landed at San Francisco International Airport. I was once again on the ground in the United States! John and I said goodbye, wished each other luck, then went our separate ways, at least for a while. We ran into each other again in one of the airport bars. We both had to wait several hours to catch our next flight to home.

While we sat there, the captain and I were joined by an Army Master Sergeant who the captain knew from somewhere they had served together. They shook hands and talked, and eventually we were introduced. I noticed that the sergeant was only wearing one ribbon, something I found odd since the rank of E8 and the service stripes on his sleeve meant he had been in the Army a long time. It took me awhile, but I finally realized that the one and only ribbon the sergeant was wearing -- a blue field with five white stars on it -- was the Congressional Medal of Honor! I had never seen one or met anyone who had one. I, of course, had seen pictures of the medal, but I guessed I had never seen the ribbon that you wear on your dress uniform to represent the award. I was in awe.

Eventually the sergeant left us to use the restroom. Cpt. Montgomery asked me if I recognized the ribbon the sergeant was wearing. I said I had, and he told me that the sergeant was returning to Vietnam for his fifth tour. Because it was his fifth tour and the fact that he was a Medal of Honor recipient, he had to have President Nixon's approval to go back.

"I don't ever want to go back again," I said. "I appreciate and respect his commitment; I do. I voluntarily joined the Army, I volunteered for Vietnam, and I volunteered for Scouts. I did my job the best I could every day. I never turned down a mission. But there is no way in hell that I would go back again."

"What if you were ordered to go back?"

"Hmm? Yeah, then there's that."

He told me what he knew of the sergeant's story, and it was right out of Audie Murphy.

He and his men had been ambushed in a convoy. He had personally manned a .50 cal machine gun, killing a lot of VC, and was responsible for saving many of his men's lives in the process. He also earned the third of his three Purple Hearts. A true hero.

The three of us spent several hours together in the airport bar, mainly talking, not really drinking, and one by one, went our separate ways. I was finally on a commercial airliner bound for Indiana and home, but I knew I would never be the same. None of us would ever be the same.

In Memoriam

20 Feb 1971	WO1 Carl Nacca Jr.	KIA AH-1G	Vietnam
22 Feb 1971	SGT Monty L. Harbin	KIA	Vietnam
10 Mar 1971	SP4 Robert T. Kiser	KIA OH-6A	Cambodia
10 Mar 1971	SGT Curtis R. Smoot	MIA/BNR OH-6A	Cambodia
17 Mar 1971	1Lt Larry E. Lilly	MIA/BNR AH-1G	Cambodia
23 Mar 1971	CW2 Paul J. Foti	KIA AH-1G	Cambodia
23 Mar 1971	1Lt Donald K. Osborn	KIA AH-1G	Cambodia
10 Apr 1971	WO1 Hugh M. Pettit	KIA UH-1H	Vietnam
7 May 1971	1Lt Frank (Walt) Bengtson	KIA OH-6A	Cambodia
7 May 1971	WO1David P. Meyer	KIA OH-6A	Cambodia
7 May 1971	SP4 Larry W. Rothel	KIA OH-6A	Cambodia
11 Jul 1971	WO1 Mike E. Lukow	KIA OH-6A	Cambodia

Vietnam Veteran Aviators in the Indiana Army National Guard

All great pilots that I flew with who decided to put the uniform back on after Vietnam

LTC George R. Belin Jr.
CW5 Jon L. Carrico
CW5 Lew E. Collier
CW5 Jess Findley
CW5 Jim Hamilton
LTC C. Neal "Doc" Heape
CW4 Darrell L Jaggers
CW4 Wallace "Bubba" Kinder
CW4 Tom Kleis
CW5 Robert "Bobby" Leonard Jr.
CW4 Paul "Felix" Miller
CW3 Thomas Miller
CW4 Robert L. Nash
CW4 Don L. Nicholas
CW5 Jack T F Pike,
CW4 Dave H. Prange
CW4 Donald G. Schneider
CW5 Bob E. Truitt
CW4 Denton R. Wilson
MG Timothy J. Wright
CW4 Chuck Yingst

If I have left someone out I am very sorry

Printed in the USA
CPSIA information can be obtained
at www.ICGtesting.com
LVHW091224300923
759526LV00002B/273

9 781958 889220